Contents

KU-360-297

About the authors

Henmans Freeth (now part of Freeths LLP; www.henmansfreeth.co.uk) has a long-established personal injury practice, handling claims nationally for both claimants and defendants, from an Oxford base. Formerly Henmans LLP, Henmans Freeth is recognised as a leading personal injury firm in the legal directories. A specialist team deals with cases, from serious brain injuries and fatal accidents to minor road traffic accidents. The bulk of the work undertaken relates to medium to large claims, arising out of accidents at work, road traffic accidents and clinical negligence.

Three members of the team have combined forces to produce this 'one stop' book for anyone responsible for health and safety issues in the workplace.

Paul Chadder is head of Henmans Freeth's personal injury department. He handles all types of personal injury claim but specialises in accidents in the workplace and public liability claims for defendants. Paul is a member of the Law Society's Specialist Personal Injury Panel. He is also the author of Lawpack's *Risk Assessment Kit*.

Mary Duncan is a former partner in Henmans LLP's personal injury department. She specialised in personal injury litigation for claimants and defendants, and professional indemnity work for defendants. For many years she was a member of the Law Society's Specialist Personal Injury Panel. She is also co-author of *Fatal Accident Litigation*, published by Fourmat Publishing (1993), and has written a chapter in *Trauma Care*, published by Butterworths (2000).

Penny Heighway is a former partner in Henmans LLP's personal injury department. She handled all types of personal injury claims, specialising in accidents at work, industrial injury cases, medical malpractice and professional indemnity work for defendants. She is a former member of the Law Society's Specialist Personal Injury Panel.

Introduction

In the last 40 years, the obligations upon and duties of an employer in the area of health and safety in the workplace have mushroomed. The combination of European legal influences and a more litigious society has led to a rise in legal claims which has left many businesses struggling to secure compulsory employer's liability insurance. Without such insurance a business is no longer able to trade.

Business owners are experts in business, not in insurance or health and safety law. This book is an attempt to explain, in a straightforward way, the legal requirements that an employer needs to comply with, in this increasingly complex area.

We would like to thank counsel, Charles Brown and Judith Ayling of 39 Essex Street, for their consideration and time in reviewing the content of an earlier edition of this book and for offering many useful comments. We would also like to thank Gemma Morris, Liz Turnbull, Amanda Shearer and Jo Eden for their assistance. The writers emphasise that any mistakes are their own and ask the reader to note that the law is correct as at 1 May 2015.

Paul Chadder
Mary Duncan
Penny Heighway

CHAPTER 1

General information

1.1 Background

Every working day, there is on average one death and 311 reported non-fatal injuries to workers. Every year, three-quarters of a million people take time off work due to work-related illness and, as a result, last year about 27 million work days were lost.

In the UK, absenteeism is costing employers approximately £14 billion a year. Small companies, where the absence of one or two employees can make a huge difference, are the hardest hit.

Employers must have insurance cover for their employees' work-related injuries and ill-health. They also need insurance for accidents involving vehicles and possibly public liability and buildings insurance. However, various changes in the last 30 years have made employer's liability insurance an unattractive class of business for insurers. With mounting losses, the only companies they want on their books are those with a genuine commitment to health and safety. Many companies are being forced out of business, unable to trade without insurance cover or because of soaring premiums. Those who have difficulty getting renewal terms have often shown a disregard for health and safety issues in the past.

However, insurance policies only cover a small proportion of the costs of accidents. Costs not covered by insurance can include the following:

- Sick pay

- Damage or loss of products and raw materials

- Repairs to the plant and equipment

- Overtime working and temporary labour

- Production delays

- Investigation time

- Criminal fines

On a more positive note, managing the well-being of employees does offer the employer a means of reducing costs and motivating the workforce.

The law states that it is an employer's duty to ensure that the risks to health and safety are properly controlled and that there is the correct provision for the employees' welfare. In certain circumstances, this responsibility extends to the self-employed and to the protection of the health and safety of other people who may be affected by your business.

It is not always easy for business owners to find out exactly what is expected of them. It is hoped that this book, which is aimed towards the small to medium-sized employer in all areas of employment from office work to heavy industry, will help you navigate the important aspects of health and safety law. This will, hopefully, ensure that not only those on your premises are protected but that you are also protected from breaking the law.

1.2 The Health and Safety Executive

In the UK, the Health and Safety Executive (HSE) is the main body responsible for enforcing legislation and providing guidance on health and safety in the workplace. The HSE comprises over 3,000 staff. As well as inspectors, there are policy, medical and scientific advisers. In addition to the HSE, more than 380 local authorities are used to enforce the relevant law. Your local fire brigade also has certain responsibilities. The shared responsibility for enforcing health and safety is split by the type of business. The enforcing bodies dealing with each type of business are listed below:

- **The HSE** covers offices, factories, building sites, mines and quarries, fairgrounds, railways, chemical plants, offshore and nuclear installations, schools and hospitals.

- **The local authority** enforcement officers cover retailing, warehouses, most offices, hotel and catering, sports, leisure and consumer services.

- **The local fire brigade** deals with fire safety.

The law grants the enforcing bodies a wide range of powers. Amongst others, they have the right to do the following:

- Enter premises at any reasonable time, or at *any* time if in their opinion there is a dangerous situation.

- Carry out examinations and investigations, take measurements, photographs and samples, take possession of articles and arrange for them to be dismantled or tested.

- Require information, take statements from people and inspect copy documents.

- Issue improvement and prohibition notices and prosecute people in companies.

A report by Professor Ragnar Löfstedt, published in November 2011, was commissioned by the government to provide an independent review of health and safety legislation. One of its various proposals questioned the HSE's role in directing inspection and enforcement activity. The HSE has since developed a risk-based enforcement code to guide local authorities in their interventions. They have also published a list of sectors and activities suitable for proactive inspection.

We will deal more fully with the role of the HSE in chapter 4, sections 2 and 5.

1.3 **Legal requirements**

Breaches of health and safety law can incur both criminal and civil liability.

Criminal liability

A crime is an offence against the state. In health and safety law, criminal liability refers to the duties and responsibilities under statute, primarily the Health and Safety at Work Act 1974 (also known as the 'HSW Act'). There are also several sets of regulations. These implement European legislation and provide the minimum health and safety requirements expected of an employer.

Both the HSW Act and the regulations are written in complicated legal jargon, so in order to help explain them in a language that is easier to understand approved codes of practice (ACOP) and guidance notes are issued regularly. The ACOP have special legal status similar to that of the Highway Code.

The penalties that can be imposed by the criminal courts include fines and imprisonment.

Civil liability

A civil action typically involves negligence and/or breach of legislation. In addition to the HSW Act and the regulations, various cases have also established legal principles which employers are obliged to follow. In a civil action a 'claimant' (the wronged person) sues a 'defendant' (the wrongdoer) for a remedy – usually financial compensation.

The question of whether a breach of a duty imposed on an employer by the regulations gives a right of action in civil proceedings is one which needs careful consideration.

For injuries sustained prior to 1 October 2013, a breach of a duty does not automatically give a person a right of action in civil proceedings against an employer, but this is often the case. It is nonetheless still necessary to consider the wording of the specific regulation.

For injuries sustained after 1 October 2013 however, the introduction of section 69(3) of the Enterprise and Regulatory Reform Act 2013 means that the regulations will not impose civil liability, unless the regulations state otherwise. Those exceptions are limited. A breach of the regulations will now be used to try and prove that an employer has acted negligently. Legal advice from a Law Society recommended solicitor should always be sought.

The Health and Safety at Work Act 1974 and regulations

The HSW Act requires the business owner to carry out actions that are reasonable and practicable in order to protect the workforce. The Act covers not only those who work full-time but also part-timers, casual workers and outside contractors. It also includes those who may use your business premises or equipment, which may include visitors and delivery drivers.

The regulations tend to relate to specific issues or risks in the workplace. We will deal with those risks commonly found in the workplace in detail in chapter 3.

It is, of course, impossible to make your premises 100 per cent safe and risk free, and both the HSW Act and regulations recognise this. As a general rule, to prosecute criminal proceedings successfully, the HSE must prove beyond reasonable doubt that the business owner failed to act as a reasonable employer in all the circumstances.

Six sets of regulations came into force in 1992 (but some of them have since been updated and are also subject to more recent amendments). They are often referred to as the 'Six Pack'. These are as follows:

- The Management of Health and Safety at Work Regulations 1999

- The Workplace (Health, Safety and Welfare) Regulations 1992

- The Provision and Use of Work Equipment Regulations 1998 (PUWER)

- The Manual Handling Operations Regulations 1992

- The Health and Safety (Display Screen Equipment) Regulations 1992 (DSE)

- The Personal Protective Equipment at Work Regulations 1992 (PPE)

There are other additional regulations. The Six Pack and other main legislation are summarised below. Many are dealt with in more detail in later chapters. It is important to know the contents of the regulations so that you are aware of your obligations and duties as an employer.

The Management of Health and Safety at Work Regulations 1999

These regulations are accompanied by an approved code of practice. You must comply with the precise terms of these regulations to avoid a potential claim for compensation.

To ensure a safe workplace these regulations state that it is the employer's responsibility to do the following:

- Carry out a suitable and sufficient assessment of the risks to the health and safety of employees in order to identify hazards, evaluate the extent of risks and take appropriate action. In addition, an employer must carry out a further assessment after an accident has occurred.

- Record the arrangements for health and safety including planning, organisation, control and monitoring as well as undertake a review of the 'protective and preventative measures' in place. Every employer must appoint one or more competent persons to assist him in undertaking these tasks.

- Employ competent people to carry out the work duties. You must not employ children of under school-leaving age, unless their employment is part of an authorised scheme.

- Ensure that any necessary contacts with external services are arranged, for example, first aid and emergency medical care.

- Provide comprehensive health and safety information to all employees, including temporary employees. This includes information on risks to health and safety as identified by risk assessments, preventative and protective measures and the identity of the competent person outlined above. Be aware of communication issues such as language differences.

- Make arrangements for the safety of employees of other companies on site and provide appropriate instructions and information.

- You should note that if fellow workers are injured as a result of another worker carrying out work for which he is untrained, the business owner can be liable.

- Provide safety training at induction, or upon transfer to a new job or area, or when new equipment is introduced. (Keep training records as evidence of this.)

- Employees are required to report any shortcomings in safety arrangements to their employers.

- Following an accident, the employer is required to complete an accident investigation (and record the findings).

- Keep records that you have undertaken all of the above.

The Workplace (Health, Safety and Welfare) Regulations 1992

These state that your premises should not be, or create, a risk to your workforce. This is not restricted to the building itself but covers four main areas:

- **Working environment:** includes temperature, ventilation, lighting and emergency lighting, room dimensions and space, suitability of workstations, seating and outdoor workstations.

- **Safety:** includes safe passage for pedestrians and vehicles. Windows and skylights must be capable of being opened, closed and cleaned safely. Transparent doors and partitions must be marked and made of safe material. There should be safety devices on doors, gates and escalators and floors must be constructed safely and be free from hazards such as slipping, tripping and obstructions. Falls from heights, dangerous substances and falling objects should be prevented by guards or safety rails. Warning signs should be placed where necessary.

- **Facilities:** there must be suitable and sufficient lavatories, washing facilities and changing areas together with storage areas and lockers for clothing. There should be adequate rest facilities and areas for eating and drinking. Drinking water must also be provided.

- **Housekeeping:** your workplace must be kept clean and maintained at all times. Spillages must be cleaned up immediately and provision must be made for the removal of waste material. You must keep housekeeping, repair and maintenance records.

The Provision and Use of Work Equipment Regulations 1998 (PUWER)

These state that in the course of carrying out their jobs, workers must be provided with machinery and equipment that is safe to use. It is important to note that employers are responsible for any injury sustained by a worker as a result of defective machinery, even if the defect arose during the manufacture of the machinery.

Work equipment is broadly defined under these regulations. It includes everything from a small screwdriver to a major plant (e.g. an oil refinery) but excludes construction sites, which are dealt with in other regulations. The general duties of an employer are to:

- consider the risks in the workplace before buying new equipment;

- provide adequate training, information and instruction on the equipment (and document as much as possible);

- ensure that the equipment is properly maintained (and keep maintenance and repair logs);

- protect the user from dangerous parts of the machinery (e.g. by fitting guards and emergency stop controls);

- reduce the danger caused by specific hazards;

- ensure the stability of the equipment, provide adequate lighting and make warnings and markings clearly visible. See chapter 3 for further information.

The Manual Handling Operations Regulations 1992

The regulations require the employer to:

- assess manual handling tasks in the workplace by way of a risk assessment (and keep copies of the assessments including post-accident assessments);

- avoid manual handling in so far as is reasonably practicable;

- mechanise the task if possible;

- reduce the risk of any injury to the lowest level reasonably practicable;
- train staff in safe methods of lifting if necessary and document all the training and information given to staff. (see chapter 3, section 2 for further information);
- provide information to staff as to the weight, or heaviest side, of the load;
- have regard to the physical suitability of staff; their clothing and footwear; the personal effects they are wearing; and their knowledge and training.

The Health and Safety (Display Screen Equipment) Regulations 1992 (DSE)

These regulations cover screens and workstations. They require the employer to:

- analyse the workstations to assess and reduce risks, and to keep copies of the assessments;
- plan work to ensure adequate breaks;
- provide information and training to users of equipment and keep documentation relating to this;
- consult on software design and selection (see chapter 3, section 4 for further information).

The Personal Protective Equipment at Work Regulations 1992 (PPE)

Personal protective equipment (PPE) is all equipment designed to protect against risks to health and safety and includes most types of equipment not covered in other legislation. PPE must be used only as a last resort, where another safer system of work cannot be implemented. If PPE is needed, it must be provided free by the employer. See chapter 2, section 8 for further information.

The Reporting of Injuries, Diseases and Dangerous Occurrence Regulations 2013 (RIDDOR)

The reporting of certain accidents and ill-health at work is a legal requirement. This is dealt with in detail in chapter 4, section 1.

The Control of Substances Hazardous to Health Regulations 2002 (COSHH)

These are often referred to as COSHH and they require an employer to:

- assess all the substances held in the workplace which are, or may be, hazardous to health (see chapter 3, section 5 for further information);

- ensure that all hazardous substances are labelled correctly with the appropriate signs;

- undertake separate assessments for PPE (see chapter 2, section 8 for further information);

- provide instruction and training in relation to PPE and training in general;

- conduct health surveillance if necessary.

The Noise at Work Regulations 1989 and Control of Noise at Work Regulations 2005

The employer is under a general duty to arrange for an adequate noise assessment and to reduce the risk of damage to the lowest level which is reasonably practicable. Special risk assessments must be undertaken. See chapter 3, section 9 for further information.

The Health and Safety (First Aid) Regulations 1981

These regulations place a general duty on the employer to make adequate first aid provision for their employees if they become injured or ill at work. See chapter 2, section 2 for further information.

The Environmental Protection Act 1990

This Act demands certification from an employer of all waste removed from a site. The purpose of the Act is to ensure the safe disposal of all waste in a proper and safe manner to an appropriate disposal site. This includes the effective disposal of waste which may seep through soil and enter the water table, as well as the removal of hazardous materials and liquid.

The Safety Representatives and Safety Committees Regulations 1977 and the Health and Safety (Consultation with Employees) Regulations 1996

Although it is unlikely to apply to a small business, if you do have union representation you must consult them on health and safety matters and in prescribed cases, appoint a safety representative and/or safety committee.

In any event, you must consult your employees on issues regarding changes affecting health and safety and the provision of information and training.

The Health and Safety Information for Employees Regulations 1989

These regulations require information relating to health, safety and welfare to be given to employees by means of posters or leaflets in the approved form. Copies of the posters and leaflets can be obtained from the HSE (see chapter 2, section 2 for further information.)

Other regulations

Other regulations which deal with health and safety issues include the Electricity at Work Regulations 1989, the Safety Signs Regulations 1996, the Lifting Operations and Lifting Equipment Regulations (LOLER) 1998 and the Work at Height Regulations 2005 which came into force on 6 April 2005.

If you are a builder or at all involved in construction, you will need to look at the Construction (Design and Management) Regulations 2007 (refer to chapter 3, section 14 for further information).

This list is not exhaustive. It is advisable to obtain full copies of the most relevant and up-to-date regulations to ensure that you comply with them. Copies can be obtained from the HSE's website at www.hse.gov.uk. It is possible to obtain some of their leaflets and publications free of charge.

CHAPTER 2

Starting a business
Initial considerations for the employer

2.1 **Registering your business**

It is no longer necessary for most employers to notify their Health and Safety Executive (HSE) inspector or local authority that they have started a commercial or industrial business that operates from factories, offices, shops (and certain railway premises) where employees work. It is considered no longer necessary because there are other systems in place that inform the HSE about the existence of factories and local authorities about office and shop premises.

However, if you work with hazardous substances or in a hazardous industry such as construction, you may need to apply for a licence or notify the HSE or your local authority.

2.2 **Providing information to employees**

You should be aware that certain health and safety information must be provided to your employees in order to comply with the law. This includes:

1. The Health and Safety Law poster/pocket card.

2. The location of first aiders and the first aid box.

3. The location of the accident book.

4. The health and safety policy document.

The health and safety law poster

It is a legal requirement that a Health and Safety Law poster is displayed in the workplace. A large A2 poster is published by the HSE and must be displayed prominently so that employees have the opportunity to familiarise themselves with the law on health and safety at work. Alternatively, a pocket card can be given to all workers. The latest version of the poster and pocket card was published on 6 April 2009, and must be used instead of the old version by no later than 5 April 2014. These posters or leaflets can be obtained directly from the HSE.

There is no longer a requirement to put contact details of health and safety representatives and the firm's enforcing authority on the poster. An employer can alternatively provide information as to how his employees may obtain this information.

First aiders

Legal considerations apart, there is clearly a case for having as many people as possible trained in basic first aid procedures. Such knowledge could be instrumental in saving the life of a person whatever the circumstances. However, the law says that you must have:

• A person in your workplace who can take charge in an emergency.

• A first aid box.

• A notice stating where the first aid box is and who the approved person is.

• A trained first aider and first aid room if your workplace gives rise to special hazards.

Once the health and safety risks associated with your particular business have been assessed (see section 4 for further information), you can consider whether you simply need to nominate a person to be responsible for first aid or whether you need to have a trained first aider. Also you will need to know what the minimum number of items in your first aid box should be, how many first aid boxes are required and where they should be located.

On the next page is a guide as to the requirements for first aiders. It is not a legal requirement. As your company grows, it is important to reassess the need for qualified first aiders.

The Health and Safety (First Aid) Regulations 1981 lay down various requirements for the provision of suitably trained first aiders in the workplace. Training courses in first aid at work should be provided by training organizations that meet the criteria laid down by the HSE. See www.hse.gov.uk/firstaid/first-aid-training.htm.

Once a course is completed, your employee holds a valid first aid at work certificate. This must be renewed every three years. A shorter updating course can then be undertaken. However, if the course is not attended before the expiry of the three years, then the employee must completely retrain.

Do remember that first aiders and people with first aid responsibility will be away from work from time to time so you need to arrange appropriate cover.

You should also be aware that the compulsory element of the employer's liability insurance does not cover litigation resulting from first aid to non-employees. However, many public liability insurance policies do cover this aspect and you may want to check your public liability insurance policy on this point.

If you have a first-aid room, it must be easily accessible to stretchers and be sign-posted.

Type of business	Number of workers	First aid provision
Lower Hazard Retail shops, offices (accountants, solicitors, etc), public buildings, car showrooms	Fewer than 25	At least one appointed person
	Between 25 and 50	At least one emergency first aider (EFAW)
	More than 50	At least one first aider at work (FAW) for every 100 employed
Higher Hazard Chemical plants/ manufacturing, building/construction sites, heavy engineering, biological plants, slaughterhouses, warehouses, food production and assembly plants	Up to 5	At least one appointed person
	Between 5 and 50	At least one first aider
	More than 50	At least one first aider for every 50 employed

The first aid box

All first aid containers must be identified by a white cross on a green background. You need to assess the level of health and safety risks your workers face as it is impossible to be definitive about what your first aid box should contain. For a business where there is no heightened level of risk to its workforce, here is a list of items that may be regarded as a minimum requirement:

- A first aid guidance leaflet.

- At least three pairs of disposable gloves.

- Four individually wrapped sterile eye pads.

- Six to eight safety pins (various sizes).

- Four sterile bandages (triangle shaped).

- Five large individually wrapped sterile wound dressings.

- 20 individually wrapped sterile adhesive dressings (various sizes), appropriate to the type of work.

- Two 5cm 5 5cm bandages.

- Two 2.5cm 5 5cm bandages.

- Ten absorbent cotton wool balls.

- One zinc oxide plaster (for securing dressings).

- 15 multi-stretch plasters (various sizes).

- Pack of antiseptic wipes.

- Tube of antiseptic cream.

- One pair of small scissors.

You should not keep tablets or medicines in the first aid box. If you use dangerous plant machinery, toxic chemicals or hazardous substances (e.g. cleaning solvents), you may require different items to be contained in your first aid kit.

In addition, you should consider whether different areas of the business premises pose a different risk to others, for example:

- How spread out are the premises?

- Are there several buildings?

- Is there more than one floor and, if so, do you need separate medical facilities on each?

Finally, if you employ people with special needs or disabilities you must consider whether these needs are catered for.

The accident book

All employees should be informed where the company's accident book is located. This could be at reception or, in larger organisations, in the first aider's room.

There are various accident record books on the market or you could maintain the record in a computer file. However you choose to document accidents, certain specific information is required:

* Details of name, age, status, job title

* Injury details: nature of accident and injury/disease

* When the accident occurred: date, time, place

The health and safety policy document

If you employ five or more employees, you must have a written health and safety policy and bring it to the attention of your employees.

According to section 2(3) of the Health and Safety at Work Act, the policy should:

* set out the employer's general policy with respect to health and safety;

* describe the organisation and arrangements for carrying out that policy;

* be reviewed as often as appropriate (e.g. annually).

Having your own policy statement is very important. Health and safety inspectors often ask to see the policy statement during inspection visits. A policy statement demonstrates that a business is committed to planning and managing health and safety. Before finalising your policy statement, it is a good idea to consult your workers. This helps to ensure that all the necessary systems and procedures are in place. It should be clear from your statement who is responsible for the different areas of the health and safety requirements. Do remember that after this policy has been written, discussed and agreed with the workers, it should be implemented!

Preparing a health and safety policy document

Often business owners find it difficult to formulate and document their policy. The following guidance therefore may be helpful in providing a template for the small business owner.

The policy should be in written form and signed and dated by the owner, occupier or person having control of the business.

Depending on the type of business, most businesses now set out their policy in three main sections:

Part 1: The statement of general policy on health and safety at work

This section describes your commitment to managing health and safety effectively, and what you want to achieve. Examples of this could be to engage and consult with employees every day or to implement emergency procedures.

Part 2: The responsibility section

This sets out who is responsible for specific actions and their duties.

Part 3: The arrangements/action section

This section contains details of what you are going to do in practice to achieve the aims set out in your statement of health and safety policy, i.e. how you are going to meet the commitments you have made in your statement, such as actions you are going to take to eliminate or reduce the risks of hazards in your workplace. This section should be customised to meet your own work situation.

Additional arrangements you can make to manage health and safety should also be set out in the arrangements section. These additional arrangements may include:

- Staff training – highlight who is responsible for training. Training records should be kept and their whereabouts noted.

- Signs to highlight risks – you can highlight where the signs are displayed.

- Anti-slip flooring.

- Replacing hazardous chemicals with less harmful alternatives – be sure to identify the hazardous chemicals and who is responsible for the detailed assessment, which is required under the Control of Substances Hazardous to Health Regulations 2002 (COSHH).

- Improved lighting.

- Improved safety equipment – this may include identifying who is responsible for the maintenance of a particular machine.

An example of a health and safety policy can be found on the HSE website.

More specific guidance

This checklist is only a guide to what you should consider including in your company's health and safety policy document. It is by no means exhaustive and different company circumstances will determine what needs to be included and what can be safely excluded.

In order to help the small business with the preparation of its own policy, the HSE has produced an excellent health and safety publication which employers can use to comply with the law. It is free and is called *Health and safety made simple*. You can download the document at www.hse.gov.uk/pubns/indg449.pdf, or call 01787 881165.

2.3 Emergency procedures

The Management of Health and Safety at Work Regulations 1999 require employers to establish 'procedures for serious and imminent danger and for danger areas'. The risk assessments required under the regulations (dealt with in detail in the next section) should identify any significant risks which arise out of the specific workplace. These may include, for example, the potential for a major escalating fire, explosion, building collapse, pollution incident and/or bomb threat.

Fundamentally, the question must be asked, 'What are the worst possible types of incident that could arise from the work undertaken in my workplace?' Once these major risks which may result in serious and or imminent danger have been identified, a formal emergency procedure or plan must be produced.

The procedures should set out the role, identity and responsibilities of the competent persons nominated to implement the action. These procedures should normally be written down, clearly setting out the limits of action to be taken by all employees. In particular, work should not be resumed after an emergency if serious danger remains. You should always consult the emergency authorities if in doubt.

In shared workplaces, separate emergency procedures should take account of others in the workplace and should, as far as is appropriate, be co-ordinated.

Fire prevention

Every year, losses to business through fire are substantial. In order to prevent death and human injury, damage to property and the consequent losses, it is essential that all your workers are familiar with the causes of fire, the fire protection procedures and the dangers associated with flammable substances. Specific training should be given on this important subject and specific information can be obtained from various external agencies. (See the Appendices for suggestions.) Training can include watching videos which can quickly and easily show employees how to cope in an emergency.

Fire appliances

Different fire appliances should be used depending on the type of fire to be tackled. For example, to douse solid materials, usually organic with glowing embers, the appropriate extinguishers are water, foam, dry powder, vaporising liquid or carbon dioxide. For liquid fires, miscible (i.e. which can be mixed) with water, the appropriate extinguishers are water, foam, carbon dioxide and/or dry powder. For liquid immiscible with water, use foam, dry power, carbon dioxide or vaporising liquid. Fire appliances introduced before 1 January 1997 are colour coded as follows:

Extinguisher	Colour code
Water	Red
Foam	Cream
Carbon dioxide	Black
Dry chemical powder	Blue
Vaporising liquid	Green

Since 1 January 1997, all fire extinguishers are (rather unhelpfully) painted red. This is due to a European Directive.

Existing extinguishers do not have to be replaced until they reach the end of their useful life. The company responsible for the maintenance of the extinguishers should make sure that, whenever possible, the two standards are not mixed to avoid confusion.

To ease the transition, British Standards allows for a coloured band at the top of the extinguisher. This is only a recommendation and throughout the UK individual manufacturers have confused matters further by colour coding in different ways! The new extinguishers have icons, indicating what type of fire they can be used on, as follows:

Classification of fire	Typical fuel	Classification icon
Class A Carbonaceous fires	• Wood • Paper • Cloth • Plastic • Rubber	
Class B Liquid fires	• Paraffin • Petrol • Types of adhesives • Types of paint • Types of spirit • Thinners	

Classification of fire	Typical fuel	Classification icon
Class C Gas fires	• Domestic gas • Butane • Acetylene • Methane	
Fires involving electricity (not a class)	Equipment: • Electric heaters • Office equipment • Electric switchboards • Electric motors • Televisions • Photocopiers • Electrically operated equipment	

	Extinguisher			
Classification of fire	Water	Carbon dioxide	Powder	Foam
A – Carbonaceous fires	Yes	Yes	Yes	Yes
B – Liquid fires	No	Yes	Yes	Yes
C – Gas fires	No	No	Yes	No
Fires involving electricity	No	Yes	Yes	No

Legal requirements

The Regulatory Reform (Fire Safety) Order 2005, came into force on 1 October 2006 (in England and Wales). The regulations state that you must carry out a fire safety risk assessment. Under the new regulations there is no separate certification system for higher risk premises and fire certificates are no longer valid.

A fire risk assessment must be carried out. You must consider all of your employees and all other people who may be affected by a fire in the workplace. You are required to make detailed provision for any disabled people, or people with special needs, who use, or may be present on, your premises (see below for more information on risk assessments; these must be recorded if you employ more than five people). The risk assessment will help you decide the nature and extent of the fire precautions that you need to provide. You must also consider:

- A means of escape in the case of fire (this excludes lifts, escalators and revolving doors). There are specific requirements as to the travel distance between any point in a building and the exit and the number of exits necessary. Specific guidance should be sought from the fire authority.

- Fire instructions must be clearly displayed, advising occupants of what action they must take on hearing the fire alarm or discovering a fire. The instructions must be displayed at prominent points in the building.

- Fire drills should result in a total evacuation of the building and should take place at least annually. Fire wardens or other designated people should take a head count on evacuation. Assembly points should be clearly identified and all persons, including visitors, should be made aware of their specific assembly point.

- The fire alarm should be sounded weekly so that all occupants of the premises are familiar with its sound.

- You must establish a suitable means of contacting the emergency services and ensure that they can be called easily.

Criminal breaches of the Regulatory Reform (Fire Safety) Order 2005 are punishable by a fine, or by a fine and imprisonment. Anyone who fails, intentionally or recklessly, to comply with the regulations and puts their employees at serious risk commits a criminal offence.

To sum up, staff should receive regular instruction in the selection and correct use of fire appliances. However, the first priority must always be to evacuate a building in the event of a fire. A good website for guidance is www.communities.gov.uk/fire/firesafety/firesafetylaw.

2.4 Risk assessments

As previously mentioned in chapter 1, you are under a legal obligation as an employer to ensure that the premises, systems of work and equipment do not pose a risk to your employees. This is dealt with in full in the Management of Health and Safety at Work Regulations 1999.

The law requires that employers ensure their employees' safety by initially undertaking a risk assessment. Do not be alarmed by the term 'risk assessment'. It is all about common sense and doing the things described in this section.

All employers are legally required to assess the risks in the workplace. If you have more than five employees, you are legally required to keep a written record of the risk assessment.

But what exactly is a risk assessment, what does it entail and what is the best way for a small business owner to go about meeting his obligations when there may be limited time and money?

What are they?

Risk

A risk is a chance, be it high or low, that someone may be harmed by a hazard. A risk assessment is a careful examination of what could cause harm to people in a particular workplace.

Hazard

A hazard means anything that can cause harm, for example, working at height or with chemicals.

Assessment

It needs to be decided whether a hazard is significant and whether it has been covered by satisfactory precautions so that the risk is greatly reduced. If it has not, it needs to be decided what precautions should be taken.

What do they entail?

In drawing up an initial outline assessment, the guiding principle is to keep things simple. In an office or commercial operation, there should not be many dangerous items or situations. It is just a combination of observation and common sense.

It is the small, often overlooked, hazards which you probably need to concentrate on. If you are a reputable employer, you will already have ensured that potentially harmful machinery is correctly guarded and your workforce has the necessary protective clothing (e.g. boots, gloves, eye protection, etc). Instead, you may have to look at the low beam at the entrance to your building or the steep inside staircase that you need to make people aware of. Taking the correct precautions may simply mean a well-placed sign. See section 9 for example signs.

If yours is a small business, then an assessment can be undertaken within the business. A larger company may wish to ask a safety representative or safety officer to assist. You could employ a private company to undertake the risk assessment on your behalf. Insurance companies will also carry out surveys to make sure that the companies they insure are up to standard. Small businesses should not view these as potential problems but effectively as free advice which can help improve things without running up professional fees.

But remember, the employer is ultimately responsible for ensuring that the risk assessment is adequately undertaken.

How to undertake an effective risk assessment

In order to assess the risks in the workplace, the following process should be undertaken.

Stage 1: Look for hazards

Spend time, ideally with a colleague, walking around your workplace with a critical eye. Think about what could go wrong at each stage of what you do. Identify and document all areas that you think may be hazardous and the type of hazards involved. If your workplace is an office, then your list will probably be short; if your workplace is a factory, it will be considerably longer. List everything, including the low beam at your entrance or the awkward staircase.

Discuss with your workforce any concerns they have and, if legitimate, add them to the list. Do not forget your own experience. Have you had any accidents? If so, document them.

Whilst it is important to document every potential hazard, you should concentrate on the ones that are significant and avoid those that are trifling. Check your accident record book to see if there are any types of injuries or accidents that recur regularly.

Stage 2: Assess who may be harmed and how

If it is the low beam outside your building, then everyone who enters is at risk. Not only are your employees in danger of hurting themselves but your visitors are also. You would not want the embarrassment of an important customer being injured whilst visiting you. New employees, who are unfamiliar with your office/shop floor/warehouse layout, will need particular attention. Likewise any person doing work experience, temporary staff or those with special needs.

Stage 3: Consider the risk and decide whether the precautions in place are adequate or whether more could be done in taking action

Ask yourself:

1. Can I get rid of the hazard altogether?
2. If not, how can I control the risk so that harm is unlikely?

Think about the following:

1. What is the worst result? For example, is it a cut finger, suffering from asbestosis or a death?
2. How likely is it to happen?

3. How many people would be affected if things did go wrong?

You should now know what the main risks in your workplace are. However, do refer to chapter 3, which covers specific risks, just to make sure that you have covered all eventualities.

If you discover a potential hazard that may endanger someone's safety and you regard it as significant, you then need to decide how best to reduce the risk. Ideally, you should eliminate the risk altogether by getting rid of the hazard but often the situation is not as clear-cut as this.

For the most part, the law requires you to do all that is reasonably practicable to ensure your place of work is safe. At the very least, you need to do everything necessary to meet the legal safety requirements and industry safety standards. If you cannot eliminate the hazard, look at ways of controlling it, for example, a non-slip mat on slippery entrance steps. Again, refer to chapter 3 on specific risks which may help you to take the correct precautions.

There may be occasions where your office is in a building occupied by other business tenants. If this is the case, then you should consult with them on any hazards that affect everyone. For example, fire escapes, reception areas, washing/toilet facilities may be areas of joint responsibility. Also, you should discuss any concerns with your landlord where the hazard relates specifically to the building and any contents that fall under the tenancy agreement.

In many instances it will be difficult to eliminate the risk and in implementing controls your main aim will be to make the risk as small as possible.

Stage 4: Document your findings

If you employ five or more people you must record the significant findings of your assessment.

You need to cover:

- The areas you have investigated.

- Any hazards you have found and whether they were significant.

- The conclusions you came to.

- The controls put in place to reduce the risks of significant hazards.

You may find it useful to include this entire document in your own health and safety policy document, which we dealt with on page 18.

Stage 5: Review the assessment and revise it as necessary

Do review the assessment, particularly following an accident at work or if new machines or substances are brought onto the site.

As your business grows, you will employ more people and invest in further, and perhaps more sophisticated equipment. When your business grows, there will also be a growth in hazards. Remember to review your assessment regularly.

Simple Generic Risk Assessment						
Premises/Work area.........						
Assessment carried out by...........						
Date of Assessment..............						
Hazard Identified	Who Is At Risk	Effect of Hazard	Existing Controls	Action Required	By When	Review Date

Example risk assessment form layout

For further information and advice on risk assessments for small to medium-size businesses, see Lawpack's *Risk Assessment Kit* available from www.lawpack.co.uk.

2.5 **Insurance provisions**

Most employers are required by law to insure against liability for personal injury or disease to their employees arising out of their employment. Recognised psychiatric or mental illness falls within the scope of personal injury. The Employer's Liability (Compulsory Insurance) Act 1969 provides that each employer should have at least a minimum level of insurance cover (£5,000,000) against any such claims. In practice, most insurance companies provide cover of £10 million or more. The Act does not grant an employee an automatic right to compensation. The purpose of the Act is to ensure that when an employee is successful in a civil claim, the employer can, through his insurer, pay the compensation that is due.

It is a legal requirement that a copy of the insurance certificate is displayed where your employees can easily read it. Since October 2008, the certificate can be displayed electronically, providing it is readily accessible by workers.

You should be aware that people who are normally thought of as self-employed may be considered employees for the purpose of employer's liability insurance. Whether insurance is required will depend upon the terms of the contract with the person. A contract may be spoken, written or implied and there are no hard and fast rules as to who counts as an employee. However, in general you may need employer's liability insurance for someone for whom you:

- deduct National Insurance and income tax from the money you pay them;
- control where and when they work and how they do it;
- supply their work materials and equipment;
- possibly share your profits, either through commission, performance pay or shares;
- require them to deliver the service and they cannot employ a substitute if they are unable to do the work;
- treat in the same way as other employees.

In general, you may not need employer's liability insurance for people who work for you if they:

- do not work exclusively for you (i.e. they work as an independent contractor);
- supply most of the materials and equipment;
- are clearly in business for their own personal benefit;
- can employ a substitute when they are unable to do the work themselves;
- do not deduct Income Tax or National Insurance.

To sum up, an employer needs employer's liability insurance unless they have people working for them who are not considered 'employees' or who are exempt.

Exempt employees are very restricted but can include those in a family business (i.e. if your employers are closely related to you, husband, wife, father, mother, grandfather, etc). However, this exemption does not apply to family businesses which are incorporated as limited companies. In some cases you will not need additional employer's liability insurance for volunteers, such as students, who work for you unpaid.

If you are in any doubt as to what is required, you should seek legal advice or consult an insurance broker. You can find a list of authorised insurers at the Prudential Regulation Authority (PRA) website (www.bankofengland.co.uk) or by telephoning them on 0207 601 4878 – see the Appendices for their contact details.

Since 1 October 2008, there has been no legal requirement for businesses to retain copies of their out-of-date insurance policies. However, it is strongly advised that employers do keep these, because the insurance covers diseases, not just accidents, which may take many years to manifest themselves; for example, mesothelioma (see the Appendices for a list of possible work-related diseases). You can keep copies electronically, if more convenient.

There are considerable fines for businesses which attempt to avoid their responsibility for providing health and safety insurance cover for their workforce. The courts do take a particularly dim view of companies without insurance, and fines of up to £2,500 can be imposed for any day on which they are without suitable insurance. Even if you simply fail to display your insurance certificate, or refuse to make it available to HSE inspectors when they ask, you may find yourself having to pay a fine of up to £1,000.

Your obligations to the insurance company

Your insurance policy is an agreement between you and your insurer concerning the circumstances in which they will pay compensation. However, your insurer cannot refuse to pay compensation to a claimant because you:

- have not provided reasonable protection for your employees against injury or disease or failed to meet a legal requirement;

- are unable to provide particular information to your insurers;

- have done something, or not done something, contrary to their instruction.

However, the policy may enable the insurer to sue you to reclaim the cost of the compensation if you do not co-operate or if you behave unreasonably. It is important to notify your insurer very promptly in the case of any accident at work, a potential claim or if the HSE notify you of a potential prosecution.

Employees abroad

Employer's liability insurance is not required to cover employees who are based abroad. However, do check the law in the country where they are based and find out if it requires you to take out insurance or carry out any other measures to protect your employees.

If any employee is normally based abroad but spends more than 14 days continuously in Great Britain or more than seven days on an offshore installation, then employer's liability insurance will be required under English law.

Other insurance policies

Any injuries or illnesses relating to motor accidents, which occur whilst your employees are working for you, may be covered separately by motor insurance. Public liability insurance covers employers for claims made by members of the public, but not for claims made by your employees. See chapter 4, section 1 for details of your obligations to report an accident to your insurer.

2.6 Recruitment and training

Your workforce is arguably the most important asset of your business. It is important to identify areas of work which place particular physical or mental demands on people. Where these demands cannot be reduced, it is important to select the right people to meet the demands. For some jobs the law requires medical examinations (e.g. for driving HGVs) but pre-employment checks are not legally required for most jobs.

The Management of Health and Safety at Work Regulations 1999 say that you have to provide health and safety training for people when they start work, when their work or responsibilities change and/or periodically if their skills are not used regularly. You should bear in mind that people returning after illness may also need help readjusting to their job. Training must be provided during working hours and not at the expense of those working for you.

When someone starts work, they will need some form of induction training. They need to know the company's safety policy and the arrangements you have made to deal with health and safety matters. Think about the needs of young and inexperienced recruits who will need a more detailed induction and be aware of special needs, such as language differences. Many of the other regulations, for example, the Provision and Use of Work Equipment Regulations 1998 (PUWER) require that you train your staff.

You should also be aware of the Equality Act 2010. The Act, which is a consolidation of all the previous discrimination law, makes it unlawful to discriminate against a disabled employee or job applicant by:

- treating him less favourably (without justification) than other employees or job applicants because of his disability; or

- not making reasonable adjustments (without justification).

We deal with this issue further in section 10 but we also suggest you either obtain a full copy of the Act from the Stationery Office (see the Appendices for details) or visit the government's website at www.gov.uk/browse/disabilities, which provides some useful guidance.

Approaches to training

'Sitting by Nellie' (i.e. learning from an experienced person on the job) can be a very effective means of training. However, it does depend on how good 'Nellie' is at passing on her skills. Nellie may also need some training on how to train!

Other forms of training include outside trainers who can be brought on site, distance learning via videotape or computer-based learning. Consider whether there are any standards of competence for what you do, for example, NVQs.

Once training has been given it is a good idea to document who has given what training, when and to whom. Training should be repeated periodically where appropriate and adapted to take into account new or changed risks.

2.7 Health surveillance

More people die from work-related diseases than from workplace accidents. The Management of Health and Safety at Work Regulations 1999 and the Control of Substances Hazardous to Health Regulations 2002 (COSHH) require health surveillance in special cases. Some jobs that require surveillance include commercial diving, work with asbestos insulation and work with chemicals. Special conditions also apply to some people, such as pregnant women, whose jobs may expose them to lead or ionising radiation.

Health surveillance means having a system to assess early signs of ill-health caused by substances and other hazards at work. It includes keeping records, organising medical examinations and testing blood and urine samples. If there are known health risks from the work you undertake, or you are in doubt, take specialist advice.

2.8 **Personal protective equipment**

Even when risks have been assessed, and controlled and safe systems of work have been applied, some risks will still remain. These could include a risk of injury to the head, for example, from falling materials; to the lungs, from breathing in contaminated air or asbestos fibres; and to the eyes, from splashes of corrosive liquid. In these circumstances, personal protective equipment (PPE) is required to reduce the risk of injury.

PPE should only be used as a last resort if there is no other way of removing the risk of injury. If PPE is still needed, it must be hygienic and otherwise free of risk to health, and provided free by the employer.

Legal requirements

The Personal Protective Equipment at Work Regulations 1992 (PPE) lay down the main requirements. However, there are special regulations which cover lead, asbestos, hazardous substances, noise and radiation. (See chapter 3, section 14 on construction for the main provisions.)

Risk assessment

If you run a small corner shop or a lawyer's practice, you may not need to consider protective clothing in any detail. However, in areas of manufacturing, construction, warehousing and distribution, there will be a risk of injury to staff.

Look for hazards

Consider:

- Who is exposed and to what?
- For how long?
- To what extent?

Reduce the risk of injury

Factors such as comfort, choice of equipment involved, ease of movement, ease of putting the item on and removing it, the effects of high temperatures and maintenance of parts are significant factors when considering the use of PPE as a means of protecting workers from hazards.

You should always take account of the health of the person who must wear the PPE. A high level of supervision and control is necessary to ensure constant use of the equipment. The employer should organise, where appropriate and at suitable intervals, demonstrations in the wearing of the PPE. Specific areas which can be protected include the following:

- **Eyes:** there may be hazards from chemical splashes, dust, gas and vapour, bright lights or radiation. Consider whether spectacles, goggles, face screens and/or helmets are necessary. Ensure that eye protection is the appropriate protection for the task. Ensure that a good quality product is bought and that the equipment suits the wearer in terms of size, fit, comfort and weight. Make sure that if more than one item of PPE is being worn, they can be used together. For example, a respirator may not give proper protection if the user is wearing safety glasses.

- **Head and neck:** beware of impact from falling or flying objects. There may also be a risk of hair entanglement or chemical drips and risks from climate or temperature (e.g. burns or frostbite). Consider helmets, hairnets, sou'westers and cape hoods. Neck protection may also be necessary, for example, during welding.

- **Ears:** refer to chapter 3, section 9 on noise. Consider earplugs or ear defenders. Only specially designed ear defenders should be fitted over safety helmets.

- **Hands and arms:** there may be a risk of cuts, punctures, chemicals, extremes of temperature, skin irritation or vibration to name a few. Consider gloves, gauntlets, mitts, wrist cuffs or armlets. Products are continually developing and you may wish to check with manufacturers on a regular basis as to whether you are using the most appropriate protection currently available. In a civil claim, where lack of PPE is alleged, you will be judged according to the types of equipment available at the time of the accident. You will also need to weigh up the risks from overheating as a result of wearing hand and arm protection (i.e. this may cause drowsiness) against the risks which are outlined above.

- **Feet and legs:** there may be a risk of slips, cuts and punctures, falling objects and chemical splashes. Consider shoes with steel toecaps, gaiters, leggings and safety boots. You will need to consider the appropriate sole pattern for the particular floor surface in your workplace.

- **Lungs:** there may be a risk from dusts, gasses and vapours. Various respirators and masks are available and specialist advice should be sought as to the most appropriate. Also consider the risks from overheating. All equipment should be suitable for its purpose and meet the necessary standards.

- **Whole body:** there may be a risk of extreme temperature, chemical splashes or clothing becoming entangled. The choice of materials for full body protection will depend upon the job in hand. Also consider other protection, for example, safety harnesses or life jackets. The HSE has now published an APC ('avoid, protect, check') approach to skin-related diseases. Guidance on this approach is available on the HSE website at www.hse.gov.uk/skin/employ/prevention.htm.

As an accident prevention strategy, the use of protective equipment relies heavily on the worker wearing the item of PPE during the whole period of time they are being exposed to the hazard. Therefore, once PPE has been provided to your employees, you should ensure that it is being worn correctly. Safety signs can be a useful reminder (see below).

General danger

 Compressed gas

 Explosive material

 Flammable material

 Oxidising material

 Corrosive material

 Dangerous for the environment

 Risk of long term health hazard such as carcinogenicity and respiratory sensitisation

 Toxic material

 Safety Helmets must be worn

 Eye protection must be worn

 Ear protection must be worn

2.9 **Signs**

Where a risk has been identified and it cannot be eliminated, it may be appropriate to fit a sign in an appropriate place. The Health and Safety (Safety Signs and Signals) Regulations 1996 encourage standardisation of safety signs throughout the member states of the European Union so that signs, wherever they are seen, have the same meaning. The sign should be maintained in good condition and kept up to date. Some signs are not immediately self-explanatory and training or instruction should be given. The law requires an employer to:

- Use road traffic signs within the workplace to regulate road traffic where necessary.

- Maintain safety signs which are provided by him.

- Explain unfamiliar signs to employees.

Examples of the most commonly used signs appear opposite.

2.10 **Special groups of workers/Equality Act 2010**

Protection of young persons

- Do not employ children under school leaving age in an industrial undertaking, except on authorised work experience schemes.

- Every employer shall ensure that young persons employed by him are protected at work from any risks that are a consequence of their lack of experience or absence of awareness due to the fact that they have not fully matured. A separate risk assessment should be undertaken.

- No employer shall employ a young person for work:

  - which is beyond his physical or psychological capacity;

  - involving harmful exposure to toxic or carcinogenic agents;

  - involving harmful exposure to radiation;

- where there is a risk to health from extreme cold, heat, noise or vibration.

The Equality Act 2010

The Equality Act aims to end the discrimination which many disabled people face. This Act gives disabled people rights in the following areas:

• Employment.

• Access to goods, facilities and services.

• Buying or renting land or property (regarding access primarily).

The Act defines a disabled person as someone with a 'physical or mental impairment which has a substantial and long-term negative effect on his ability to carry out normal day-to-day activities'.

You may need more information on who is likely to be covered by this Act. Guidance has been provided by the Office for Disability Issues. A copy of this guidance can be found on the Office for Disability Issues website. (www.odi.dwp.gov.uk).

The Equality Act 2010 – employment provisions

• As stated the provisions, which consolidate all previous discrimination legislation, have been in force since October 2010.

• There are two ways in which an employer may unlawfully discriminate against a disabled employee or job applicant:

- by treating him less favourably (without justification) than other employees or job applicants because of his disability; or

- by not making reasonable adjustments (without justification).

There is a helpful guide to the provisions contained in the Equality Act on the Office for Disability Issues website.

The Equality Act 2010 – access to goods and services

- Since October 1999, companies that provide services have had to consider making reasonable adjustments to the way they deliver their services so that disabled people can use them.

- Since October 2004, service providers have had to consider making permanent physical adjustments to their premises if it would otherwise be unreasonably difficult for disabled people to use their services.

Under the Workplace (Health, Safety and Welfare) Regulations 1992, recent amendments state that adequate seating must be provided in rest areas for the number of disabled persons at work. In addition, all parts of a workplace used or occupied directly by disabled persons at work must be organised to take into account their needs.

The Equality and Human Rights Commission and the Disability Unit at the Department for Work and Pensions (see the Appendices for their contact details), through their helpline and website, provide information and advice both to disabled people on their rights and to service providers on their duties under the Equality Act.

2.11 **New or expectant mothers**

In many workplaces there are hazards which may affect the health and safety of new and expectant mothers, and that of their children. There are specific laws which require employers to protect the health and safety of these employees.

Legal requirements

The Management of Health and Safety at Work Regulations 1999 apply, as does the Equality Act 2010. If an employer fails to protect the health and safety of their pregnant workers, it is automatically considered to be discrimination.

Risk assessment

The employer is required to conduct a risk assessment for his employees which should also include any specific risks to females of childbearing age who **could** become pregnant and any risks to new and expectant mothers. New mothers include those who have given birth within the previous six months or who are breast-feeding.

Look for hazards

Your employees must inform you that they are pregnant or breast-feeding. Until you have received written notification, you are not obliged to take any action other than those resulting from the risk assessment for all employees, mentioned above.

Once you have received notification, consider whether the employee may be at risk from different physical, biological and chemical agents, working conditions and processes.

Some of the more common risks may be as follows:

- The lifting or carrying of heavy loads.
- Standing or sitting for long periods of time.
- Exposure to infectious diseases, lead, radioactive material and smoke in the workplace.
- Work-related stress.
- Workstations and posture, as well as long working hours.
- Excessive noise.

Consider whether it is possible to remove or reduce the risk. For example, can the working conditions or hours of work be adjusted, or can the employee be given suitable alternative work on the same terms and conditions?

As an employer you will need to regularly monitor and review any assessment made to take into account the possible risks which may occur at the different stages of pregnancy. If it is not possible to reduce or eliminate the risk, then an employer must suspend an employee from work on paid leave for as long as is necessary to protect the health and safety of the employee and/or her child.

2.12 **Working time**

Working time is the time spent during your working hours which includes rest breaks. It is now controlled by legislation.

The Working Time Regulations 1998 impose obligations on employers in relation to the working time of workers over the minimum school-leaving age, including the provision of rest breaks and night work restrictions. The HSE and your local authority are the enforcing authorities.

The regulations apply to most (but not all) workers. For example, training doctors are excluded.

The regulations provide that:

- Workers must not work for more than an average of 48 hours per seven-day week, calculated over a 17-week period.

- Travelling to work is not included, unless travel is part of the job.

- Workers can agree to work more than a 48-hour week but the agreement must be:

  - in writing;

  - in relation to a specified period or apply indefinitely;

  - terminable by the worker by seven days' notice given to the employer.

- The normal working hours of night workers must not exceed an average of eight hours in a 24-hour period. (There are, however, exceptions, e.g. surveillance or security workers.)

- The Working Time (Amendment) Regulations 2009 came into force on 1 August 2009. These Regulations amend the working time limit for certain doctors in training from 48 hours to 52 hours until 31 July 2011.

The first criminal prosecution under the Working Time Regulations took place in 2002. The prosecution was against a newsagents, for failing to limit an employee's hours to an average of 48 per week. The employee involved had worked up to 97 hours per week and was awarded £1,200 compensation. The company was fined £5,000 and ordered to pay £2,150 costs. These prosecutions may become more common.

See chapter 3, section 15 for information on tachographs and the legal restrictions on driving times and breaks.

2.13 **Agency workers**

Under the Conduct of Employment Agencies and Employment Businesses Regulations 2003, employment agencies and employment businesses have specific legal responsibilities to provide information to businesses who use their workers.

Agency workers can face particular problems because, for example, they may not be familiar with the business they are working in or its particular hazards.

If you provide agency workers, you should ensure that the user business has carried out a risk assessment and given you the findings which you should pass on to agency workers. You may need to assess the risks workers face in the user business workplace before you place workers with that business for the first time. You will most likely need to do this if you are providing workers for higher-risk industries, such as construction.

When a business uses agency workers both the business and the agency have a shared duty to protect their health and safety. Agency workers could be considered your employees for health and safety purposes, even if they are not for tax and National Insurance.

It is important for both the user business and the agency to clarify and agree at the start of a contract the practical arrangements for day-to-day supervision, direction and control of the work agency workers will be doing.

If agency workers are on your site, your risk assessment needs to take them into account. You need to take into account special problems they may face, for example, any language needs. You need to ensure that they understand the information and instructions they need to work safely and that they have had any necessary training. You need to agree with the agency any arrangements for providing necessary health surveillance, computer screen eyesight tests, maintaining or providing personal protective equipment and agree an arrangement for reporting relevant accidents to the enforcing authority.

The Agency Workers Regulations 2010 and Agency Workers (Amendment) Regulations 2011 came into force on 1 September 2011. These require that agency workers be given the same rights by the hirer as if they were employees, following a qualifying period of 12 weeks.

For further guidance on the obligations of employment agencies and employment businesses, go to www.hse.gov.uk.

CHAPTER 3

Specific problems in the workplace
and how to deal with them

3.1 Slipping and tripping

Slipping and tripping injuries are the single most common cause of injuries at work, costing employers over £512 million a year in lost production and related costs. The increasingly litigious nature of society is escalating slip and trip claims to an astronomical level. Solicitors are continually dealing with claims following slips on wet leaves in poorly lit car parks, on ice from leaking gutters and from spillages on the shop floor. These are all accidents which can easily be avoided. In one claim, a customer at a hairdressers succeeded in recovering damages after she slipped on an icy entrance step. The owner was found to have been negligent in not putting down salt, as the icy weather had been forecast.

Legal requirements

The Workplace (Health, Safety and Welfare) Regulations 1992 and the Management of Health and Safety at Work Regulations 1999 require employers to provide a safe workplace where floors, corridors and stairs are free from obstruction and debris. Outdoor routes must also be kept safe, particularly during wet and icy conditions. Precautions should also be put in place to prevent either people or materials falling. The Occupier's Liability Act 1957 also requires employers as occupiers to take reasonable care that anyone invited or permitted to be on their premises is reasonably safe.

Risk assessment

Look for hazards

Some of the most common types of accident in the working environment are caused by the following:

- Trailing cables
- Cardboard boxes causing obstruction
- Badly lit stairways and corridors
- Damaged floor coverings
- Spilt drinks

Reduce the risk of injury

- Maintain equipment to stop leaks.
- Employees should be told specifically that they must let the office manager or health and safety officer know of any of the above hazards as soon as possible.
- Floors should be in good condition and free from any obstructions. Clean regularly using the right methods and products.
- You may need to use separate routes for pedestrians and vehicles.
- Repair any uneven surfaces, holes or broken boards. Inspect them regularly and keep records.
- All areas including car parks and outside routes should be kept clean and records kept of inspection, cleaning and maintenance procedures.
- When floors are cleaned, ensure a slippery floor sign is clearly

displayed. Even if you employ cleaning contractors, you will still have an obligation to your own staff.

- Increase the grip of an existing floor by treating it with non-slip paint or etching.

- Ensure that employees are wearing the correct footwear if special footwear is necessary. If this is the case, you must pay for it.

- Ensure that there is an adequate level of lighting, including outside lights. Fittings and levels of lighting should be assessed regularly.

- Ensure that there are handrails on the stairs and ramps where necessary.

- Ensure that doors are safe. For example, consider fitting vision panels on swing doors.

- Clean up spillages immediately. Not only should spillages be cleaned promptly, it is vital that other employees are alerted to the fact that there is an area of slippery floor.

- If in-house repairs are insufficient consider contacting an expert, for example, the floor manufacturer, a specialist contractor or other health and safety expert.

- Ensure that the stair coverings and treads are in good repair.

- Think about marking steps and kerbs with black and yellow diagonal stripe tape.

- Ensure that there are arrangements in place to clear ice and snow, for example, putting down salt in cold weather.

- Specific guidance is provided for areas of particular risk (e.g. where the floor may become wet from condensation) from the British Standards Institution (also known as the BSI Group). They also provide guidance on lighting, stair/step measurements and managing risks generally (see the Appendices for their contact details).

3.2 **Manual handling**

A third of accidents reported at work are associated with manual handling. Manual handling covers a wide range of activities from pushing a wheelie bin to working at a checkout. It is defined as 'supporting or transporting loads by bodily force'. Many manual handling injuries build up over a period of time rather than being caused by a single handling accident.

Legal requirements

The employer's legal duties to prevent manual handling accidents are primarily found in the Manual Handling Operations Regulations 1992 (as amended in 2002). The regulations include the following:

- Employers must take all appropriate measures to avoid the need for any manual handling.

- Risks to employees must be assessed and where manual handling is unavoidable appropriate measures must be taken to minimise the risk of injury, particularly back injury.

- Planning and control. Managers and supervisors must devise and apply safe systems of working practice. They must also ensure that the right equipment and environment is provided. Load details, for example, the weight and which way up the load should be carried, should be given.

  Employers must consider maintenance work including emergency maintenance. In one case, a worker was carrying out necessary maintenance work on a conveyor system and had to remove a roller. The worker thought the roller would be hollow but it was solid and weighed around 20 kilograms. As he removed the last bolt, it trapped his hand causing an injury. As no assessment had been undertaken and no information had been provided to the worker, the employer was liable.

- Staff must be trained in the appropriate correct methods of handling and be shown how to recognise dangerous practices.

- Employers must have regard to an employee's physical suitability; his clothing or footwear; the personal effects being worn; and his knowledge and training.

- Employees must be monitored for injuries and immediate remedial procedures must be put in place to reduce any new risks as they are identified.

- Employees must co-operate with employers and use the equipment and systems of work provided.

Risk assessment

Look for hazards

In undertaking the risk assessment, various aspects need to be looked at:

The task

Does it involve:

- The support and movement of a load?
- Frequent or prolonged effort?
- Twisting or stooping?
- Insufficient rest or recovery?

The load

Is the load:

- Heavy, sharp, hot or damaged?
- Bulky, unwieldy or difficult to grasp?
- Unstable or the contents likely to shift?

The working environment

Are there:

- Extremes of temperature or humidity?
- Space constraints preventing good posture?
- Uneven, unstable or slippery floors?

The individual employee's capability

Does the job:

- Require unusual strength or height and is the employee physically suitable to carry out the operation?

- Require special clothing or footwear?

- Create a hazard to those with health problems?

- Require special knowledge or training?

All employees should be trained in safe lifting techniques. A booklet, entitled *Manual Handling at Work,* deals with safe lifting and can be obtained from the Health and Safety Executive (HSE). The guidelines published in connection with the Manual Handling Operations Regulations 1992 provide guidance on the maximum lifting weights. As the HSE points out, there is no such thing as completely 'safe' manual handling but working within the above guidelines will reduce the risk and the need for a more detailed assessment. See the diagrams on pages 53–55 which show how men and women can lift safely.

Please note that the weights in the diagrams do assume that the load is readily grasped with both hands and that the operation takes place in reasonable working conditions with the lifter in a stable body position.

Reduce the risk of injury to the lowest level practicable

This means reducing the risk until the cost of any further precautions in time, trouble or money would be far too great in proportion to the benefits. This may include considering the following:

- **Task improvements:** this will include improving the layout of the task, the work routine and the work method, as well as reducing repetitive movements.

- **Changes to the load:** the load may be lighter, smaller, easier to manage, easier to grip, more stable and less damaging to hold.

- **Working environment:** consider space constraints, the floor and other aspects of the working environment.

- **Individual selection:** consider age, gender, health, fitness and the strength of an individual.

- **Mechanical assistance:** this would include the use of hand tools and mechanical lifting equipment.

- **Protective equipment:** for example, for hands and feet.

- **Training:** see the diagram below for the correct lifting technique. Leaflets including this information can be given to employees. Safe lifting needs to be planned. Employees must be trained to consider the following:

  - What they are lifting.

  - Its weight.

  - Its centre of gravity.

  - How to attach a load to the lifting machinery.

  - Who is in control of the lift?

  - The safe limits of the equipment.

- **Reporting:** encourage the reporting of aches and pains.

General risk assessment guidelines

- Each box in the diagram above shows guideline weights for lifting and lowering.

- Observe the activity and compare it to the diagram. If the lifter's hands enter more than one box during the operation, use the smallest weight. Use an in-between weight if the hands are close to a boundary between boxes. If the operation must take place with the hands beyond the boxes, make a more detailed assessment.

- The weights assume that the load is readily grasped with both hands.

- The operation takes place in reasonable working conditions with the lifter in a stable body position.

- Any operation involving more than twice the guideline weights should be rigorously assessed even for very fit, well-trained individuals working under favourable conditions.

- There is no such thing as a completely 'safe' manual handling operation but working within the guidelines will cut the risk and reduce the need for a more detailed assessment.

Lifting techniques

- **Place the feet apart** giving a balanced and stable base for lifting with the leading leg as forward as is comfortable.

- **Adopt a good posture.**

- Bend the knees.

- Keep hands level with waist.

- Lean forward a little over the load.

- Keep the back straight (tucking in the chin helps).

- Keep shoulders level facing the same direction as the hips.

- **Get a firm grip.**

- Try to keep arms within the boundary formed by the legs.

- **Don't jerk.**

- Carry out the lifting movement smoothly, keeping control of the load.

- **Move the feet.**

- Don't twist the trunk when turning to the side.

- **Keep the load close** to the trunk.

- Keep the heaviest side of the load next to the trunk.

- If a close approach to the load is not possible, try sliding the load towards you before attempting to lift it.

- **Put the load down, then adjust.**

- If precise positioning of the load is necessary, put it down first, then slide it into the desired position.

3.3 Upper limb disorders

The term 'upper limb disorders' covers a whole range of problems affecting the neck down to the fingers, from tennis elbow, carpal tunnel syndrome, tenosynovitis to generalised repetitive strain injury. They include such unusually named conditions as vibration white finger, golfer's elbow and gamekeeper's thumb.

There have been many cases concerning the extent to which various upper limb disorders are attributable to problems in the workplace. It is generally accepted that many may be caused, or at least made worse, by certain types of work. Much depends on the working conditions, as well as an individual's medical history and susceptibility. Upper limb disorders can give rise to severely disabling symptoms, which can seem relatively trivial at first, but should be taken seriously.

In one case, a solicitor's firm was found to have been negligent and the claimant, a legal secretary, received over £85,000 in damages when she suffered a repetitive strain injury to her hands and wrists. The judge found that there were inadequacies with her workstation but that there were other contributory factors including tight deadlines, a heavy workload, poor posture, absence of proper breaks and no change in routine. The claimant was unable to continue with typing work due to her condition.

Legal requirements

The employer is required to assess risks by the Management of Health and Safety at Work Regulations 1999. There are no specific regulations but much guidance has been provided by the HSE and others. You should also refer to the next section on VDUs as there is some overlap between these two areas.

Risk assessment

Look for hazards

It is important to look at the duration of routine tasks requiring dexterity or arm movements, the number of repetitions, the force used and the posture adopted by the employee. For example, any employee carrying out routine copy typing all day may well be at risk if action is not taken.

Production line work is often very repetitive, with limited opportunities for breaks unless these are specifically organised. Look for work particularly involving hammering, gripping, twisting, reaching and squeezing. Are there any actual cases of upper limb disorders among the workforce or complaints of problems in upper limbs?

In the case of office workers, see the useful diagrams on pages 60 and 61 concerning posture and lighting and check whether each workstation complies with the recommendations.

Reduce the risk of injury

Once it has been decided that there is potentially a risk, the following action may be taken:

- Altering the office workstations to comply with the HSE's recommendations.
- Varying the work and alternating different types of work.

- Job rotation.

- Organising breaks and ensuring these are taken.

- Assessing and, if necessary, redesigning workstations.

- Checking each employee's individual posture and seeing how awkward positions can be avoided, for example, by providing steps or more space.

- Considering whether part of the process can be automated further.

- Providing better tools.

- Ensuring that the necessary retraining is given.

- Reducing time pressures if the workforce agrees, for example, by removing piecework/bonus schemes.

- Allowing self-pacing by workers if possible, rather than speed being dictated by machines.

- Ensuring better lighting. (This may avoid employees adopting awkward positions in order to see better.)

- Providing a warm environment if possible, or at least adequate protective clothing.

- Providing training in skills, posture, and warning symptoms for those at risk.

- Providing medical surveillance for those at risk and encouraging the reporting of symptoms.

Hand-arm vibration

If someone is exposed to too much vibration, for example, through using chain saws, hand-held power tools or road drills, they may develop hand-arm vibration syndrome. This is a group of symptoms – the best known being vibration white finger. There may be loss of sensation in the fingers, reduced dexterity, pain and increased sensitivity to cold. Continued use of power tools after symptoms start will mean that the symptoms will progressively worsen and may become irreversible. There is a risk of problems if, for example, the use of tools causes tingling or numbness, either during use or immediately after.

See Section 3.10 on vibration for the legal requirements. Many of the general comments relating to upper limb disorders apply here. There are some further specific considerations. Action to take also includes the following:

- Ensuring that tools are purchased with vibration control built in.

- Ensuring that employees take regular breaks.

- If there are existing problems, then cutting down the use of power tools as far as possible and looking at whether the job can be done another way.

- Ensuring that the tools are well maintained, as this should minimise the vibration produced.

- Keeping employees warm as far as possible, or at least providing gloves.

- Training employees to warm up and exercise their fingers in order to improve blood flow.

- Ensuring employees are trained to recognise symptoms and understand the importance of reporting these to avoid more serious problems developing.

- Creating a system of health surveillance may be appropriate.

3.4 **VDUs**

Visual display units or display screen equipment are commonplace in offices, normally as computer screens. Health risks posed by VDUs include the following:

- Postural, musculo-skeletal problems including upper limb disorders.

- Eye strain/discomfort.

- Headaches.

- Fatigue and stress.

- Flickering screens may affect some epileptics.

- In unusual circumstances, skin problems, possibly due to a combination of dry air, electrostatic charge and an individual's predisposition to such problems.

There has previously been controversy regarding the association between VDU usage and pregnancy or birth defects, but the official view of the HSE in the UK is that a risk does not exist. The Health and Safety (Display Screen Equipment) Regulations 1992 (DSE) require that pregnant women should be able to discuss any concerns with a knowledgeable person.

See also the previous section on upper limb disorders as many of the comments there also apply to VDUs.

Legal requirements

The Health and Safety (Display Screen Equipment) Regulations 1992 (DSE) require that employers do the following:

- Carry out risk assessments relating to relevant employee workstations. Relevant employees, generally, are those who habitually use VDUs as a significant part of their normal work.

- Ensure that workstations meet minimum requirements as set out in the regulations.

- Ensure that there are regular breaks in the work/changes of activities.

- On request, arrange and pay for eyesight tests and provide glasses if special ones are required.

- Provide health and safety training and information to employees.

The Workplace (Health, Safety and Welfare) Regulations 1992 also apply.

Risk assessment

Look for hazards

Careful assessment of the working conditions is needed and quite a high level of detailed consideration required. Certainly in an office environment there is considerable overlap with any assessment relating to the risk of upper limb disorders.

Seating and posture for typical office tasks

1. Seat back adjustability

2. Good lumbar support

3. Seat height adjustability from the seated position

4. No pressure on underside of thighs, knees and backs

5. Foot support for smaller users

6. Space to enable and encourage postural change

7. Forearms approximately horizontal

8. Minimal extension, flexion or deviation of wrists

9. Screen height and angle should allow comfortable head position

Lighting for typical office tasks

1. **Screen:** Readable and stable image, adjustable, glare free

2. **Keyboard:** Usable, adjustable, key tops legible

3. **Work surface:** Should allow flexible arrangement, be spacious and glare free. Document holder used if appropriate

4. **Work chair:** Appropriate adjustability plus foot rest

5. **Leg room** and clearances to facilitate postural change

6. **Lighting:** Provision of adequate contrast, no direct or indirect glare or reflections

7. **Distracting noise** minimised

8. **No excessive heat,** adequate humidity

9. **Software** appropriate to the task and adapted to user capabilities. Should provide feedback on system status

Example display screen equipment assessment record

Workstation Assessment

Company Name	City Housing Association
Location	Building Services
User Name	Joanna Bloggs
Job Description	Tenant Liaison Officer

Remedial Measures Necessary	Confirmation of Action Taken	Date Action Taken
Replace the broken footrest. User to monitor her workstation comfort as pregnancy progresses and report any subsequent problems.		

Assessment Date	Signature of User	Signature of Assessor

Example display screen equipment assessment record (continued)

WYG Management Services
part of the **WYG** group

Areas to be Covered		✓ ✗	Assessors Comments
1.	Is the display screen equipment used for more than 2 hours in a working day?	✓	7 hours per day.
Display Screen			
2.	Is the image on your screen clear and easy to read?	✓	
3.	Is the screen positioned at the correct height and distance?	✓	
4.	Can the screen be swivelled and tilted?	✓	
5.	Is the image on the screen free from flicker?	✓	
6.	Are there any distracting reflections or glare?	✗	
7.	Is the screen damaged?	✗	
8.	Is the screen clean and does the user have access to cleaning materials?	✓	
Keyboard			
9.	Is the keyboard separate from the screen?	✓	
10.	Is the keyboard tiltable?	✓	
11.	Is there sufficient space in front of the keyboard for hands / arms?	✓	
12.	Is the keyboard undamaged and are the keys clear?	✓	
Other Input Devices			
13.	Is the mouse / trackball within easy reach so that the user does not have to stretch to use it?	✓	Mouse used.
14.	Does the mouse / trackball run smoothly?	✓	
Work Chair			
15.	Is the chair adjustable in height?	✓	
16.	Is the backrest adjustable in height and tilt?	✓	
17.	Is the chair a swivel type with 5 or more casters?	✓	

Example display screen equipment assessment record (continued)

WYG Management Services
part of the **WYG** group

Work Surface and Desk			
18.	Is there sufficient space to carry out required tasks and to allow for changes in posture?	✓	
19.	Is the workstation so arranged as to avoid sitting in a twisted position?	✓	
20.	Is the desk surface matt / non-reflecting?	✓	
21.	Is the desk undamaged and at the right height?	✓	
22.	Is the desk / work surface tidy and organised?	✓	
Accessories			
23.	Is a document holder provided? If not, does the user require one?	✗	Not required.
24.	Is a mouse mat provided?	✗	Not required.
25.	Is a footrest provided? If not, does the user require one?	✓	Footrest is broken and needs replacing.
26.	Are wrist rests provided? If not, does the user require them?	✗	Not required.
Work Arrangements			
27.	Does the user vary screen based and non-screen based tasks?	✓	
28.	Has the user been trained in the use off the relevant software?	✓	
29.	Has the user been trained in furniture adjustment, good posture and the DSE Regulations?	✓	
30.	Is the user aware of how to report problems and to whom?	✓	Would report any problems to her line manager.
31.	Does the user use a laptop?	✗	
32.	If yes, does the user have a docking station and separate keyboard?	n/a	
Health			
33.	Is the user aware of the need to report health problems immediately and to whom?	✓	Would report any problems to her line manager.
34.	Does the user have any health problems at the moment which may be related to the use of DSE?	✗	The user is pregnant and is currently comfortable at her workstation. User to monitor this situation as pregnancy progresses and report any subsequent problems.
35.	Is the user aware of the eye-sight testing policy?	✓	

Reproduced by the kind permission of the WYG Group

A useful basic form to assist with this risk assessment appears on pages 62–64. More detailed forms are available, for example, from the Royal Society for the Prevention of Accidents (RoSPA) – for their address, see the Appendices. Also, you may wish to ask each user to assess his workstation at the beginning of a review. This should show any area where urgent action is required.

Reduce the risk of injury

Action may include the following:

- Reviewing each employee's posture whilst at the workstation and adjusting the equipment accordingly.

- Scheduling regular breaks and ensuring that they are taken.

- Providing/ensuring variety in the work undertaken.

- Providing free eye tests and glasses if needed because of VDU work.

- Ensuring that the screens have adjustable brightness and contrast controls (compulsory since 1996).

- Ensuring that no bright lights are reflected in the screen and that the screen does not face bright lights or windows.

- When using a mouse, place the mouse close so it can be used with a relaxed arm and straight wrist.

- Ensure regular warnings are given to employees about the risks we have highlighted.

Revised guidelines, entitled *Working with VDUs*, were first published by the HSE in June 2003. They can be obtained directly from the HSE.

3.5 **Hazardous substances**

Many substances are potentially hazardous to health, from asbestos to prawns, causing health problems from mesothelioma to prawn blower's asthma. This is a large topic and any employer working with chemicals and other potentially hazardous substances to any great extent should seek specialist advice, if not an expert.

Hazards may often be partly hidden, for example, asbestos pipe lagging in older buildings. If in doubt, an expert assessment should be made. There are cases where women have developed asbestos-related fatal conditions, such as mesothelioma, where there has been no apparent contact with asbestos in the workplace. However, on further investigation, it was proven that they had been exposed to asbestos when they had placed their husband's overalls in their washing machines.

At the end of this section, the question of smoking in the workplace and asbestos-related illness will be dealt with separately.

Legal requirements

The Control of Substances Hazardous to Health Regulations 2002 (COSHH) and the new REACH Regulations (see page 70) are the principal regulations in this area. Some substances (e.g. lead, ionising radiation and explosives) are covered by specific regulations and are not dealt with in detail here. See the regulations in the Appendices at the end of the book. Regulations covering suppliers of chemicals and the carriage of dangerous goods are also beyond the scope of this book.

The employer needs to follow seven steps:

1. Assess the risks to health arising from hazardous substances in the workplace.

2. Decide what precautions are needed.

3. Prevent or adequately control exposure.

4. Ensure that control measures are used and maintained.

5. Monitor the exposure of employees to hazardous substances, if necessary.

6. Carry out appropriate health surveillance where necessary.

7. Ensure that employees are properly informed, trained and supervised.

Risk assessment

The health and safety policy should list the people responsible for COSHH risk assessments, the review period and the names of others who help to implement the action required.

For an example basic form for an initial COSHH risk assessment, see the following page.

Look for hazards

The main source of information on the qualities of any substance in the workplace is likely to be the supplier. Read the label and any data sheet. If a data sheet has not been supplied, the supplier should supply one on request. Then consider whether any of the possible hazards are likely to arise in the workplace, generally or in any particular circumstance. Then review the existing controls and consider whether anything further should be done.

A statement in a health and safety policy following a risk assessment relating to a standard office building may read as follows:

'In accordance with the COSHH Regulations, an assessment has been carried out of the possible dangers of using various substances at work. It is concluded that the only dangerous substances are:

- **Toner:** used in photocopiers, printers and fax machines. In case of spillage, do not inhale the fine powder; in case of skin contact, wash with soap and water; in case of eye contact, treat as a foreign body.

- **Bleach and similar cleaning products:** stored in our cleaning cupboards. These can only be used by staff under the supervision of the health and safety officer or office manager.

- **Tippex and thinners:** it is considered that the likelihood of anyone suffering harmful effects from exposure is low and only likely to happen if the substances were to be used in some unusual way. To avoid any risk, please use these substances at work strictly in accordance with the manufacturer's instructions'.

COSHH Risk Assessment

Premises/work area: Date of assessment:

Assessment carried out by: Position:

Material	
Chemical component	
Quantity used	
Form of supply/use	
Information from suppliers: Available Adequate	
Internal date sheet prepared	
Main hazard present (gas, vapour, fume, liquid, dust, etc)	
Summary of hazard (including effect)	
Hazard identified	
Who is at risk?	
Existing controls	
Action required	

Review date:

Signed:

Then details would follow of the people responsible under the COSHH Regulations for risk assessments and the implementation of any action, as well as details of the review period.

Other substances potentially occurring in an office environment may include ozone from photocopiers. The maintenance of the air conditioning also needs to be kept up to date.

Reduce the risk of injury

Following the risk assessment, action may be needed. Remember that exposure should be prevented if at all possible. If not possible, then it must be controlled. Action may include:

- Ensuring that clear labelling is present on all containers. Hazardous substances must be marked with a black and orange label.

- Ensuring that clear signs are present warning of hazards. See the examples in chapter 2, section 9.

- Providing suitable containers for all substances, including waste materials that may give off fumes for example, and ensuring that they are covered when appropriate.

- Considering a substitute for a substance, for example, if a chemical is flammable, looking for one with a higher flash point; if carcinogenic, looking for one that is not known to be carcinogenic.

- Reducing the amount used.

- Reducing the amount of contact an employee has with the substance.

- Providing good washing and changing facilities.

- Providing protective clothing, for example, to prevent contact with the skin or the inhalation of fumes.

- Not allowing smoking/drinking/eating in a chemical handling area.

- Reminding employees not to put pens and pencils in their mouth; this may transfer chemicals to their mouth in the process.

- Using a pump or hand-operated siphon to move chemicals.

- Controlling access.

- Taking fire precautions.

- Ensuring that substances are stored in accordance with the manufacturer's recommendations. If they are flammable, keeping them in secure storage with regulated temperature and ventilation, away from sources of ignition.

- Storing gas cylinders with valves uppermost, away from the main workplace, on the outside of the building if possible, above ground level. Also moving them in a way that minimises damage; using correct hoses, etc for the cylinder; turning off cylinder valves at the end of the day; changing cylinders in a well ventilated place; never using flame to test for leaks but using detergent/water solution instead; training welders in correct working procedures; fitting non-return valves and flame arresters; and ensuring sufficient ventilation.

- Ensuring regular cleaning. If dust is a problem, using a 'dust free' method, for example, a vacuum system with an efficient filter.

- If the plant atmosphere could be flammable, avoiding dust build up, using exhaust ventilation, controlling sources of heat and reducing any sparking.

- Improving ventilation.

- Informing and training all employees and keeping this under review.

Once action has been decided on and implemented, it must be maintained and kept under regular review at five-yearly intervals, if not more frequently.

REACH Regulations

REACH stands for Registration, Evaluation, Authorisation and Restriction of Chemicals. The REACH Regulations came into force on 1 June 2007 and they affect manufacturers and importers of substances; they are enforced by the REACH Enforcement Regulations 2008.

Manufacturers and importers are required to register substances with the European Chemicals Agency (ECHA) in Helsinki. If they do not do so, they will no longer be able to legally manufacture or supply the chemicals. These regulations only apply if you manufacture or supply one ton per year or more and there are certain exclusions. Pre-registration began on 1 June 2008. All manufacturers and importers must have been registered by 1 December 2008. Information on registration can be found on the ECHA website (http://echa.europa.eu).

The regulations affect any businesses using chemicals, which will probably include most businesses in some way or another (known as 'downstream users'). They have a duty to use chemicals in a safe manner and according to the information on risk management measures that should be passed down the supply chain. Downstream users may need to supply risk assessments and risk management measures to the European Chemicals Agency. Some users may also be importers and have a duty to register.

Businesses that sell chemicals have specific duties to pass information down to their customers and also to pass information back to their own suppliers when customers ask them to do so.

REACH will apply in addition to COSHH and the regulations are intended to result in improved information being sent down the supply chain about the hazards and risks posed by chemicals.

Smoking

Since 1 July 2007 virtually all enclosed public places and workplaces in England have become smoke free.

Smoke-free legislation is set out in part 1 of the Health Act 2006. The Act sets out the broad provisions for smoke-free legislation. The Smoke-Free Regulations made under the Health Act 2006 are as follows:

- The Smoke-Free (Premises and Enforcements) Regulations 2006

- The Smoke-Free (Signs) Regulations 2012

- The Smoke-Free (Exemptions and Vehicles) Regulations 2007

- The Smoke-Free (Penalties and Discounted Amounts) Regulations 2007

- The Smoke-Free (Vehicle Operators and Penalty Notices) Regulations 2007

The above ensure that nearly all workplaces and enclosed public places (including public transport and vehicles used by more than one person for work) must be smoke-free. This legislation came into force in England on 1 July 2007. Similar legislation took effect in Wales on 2 April and Northern Ireland on 30 April 2007. Following the introduction of the smoke free legislation it is not possible to have smoking rooms in the workplace.

From 1 October 2015, smoking will also be banned in private vehicles with passengers under 18, except in convertibles.

No-smoking signs

The regulations require that all smoke-free premises display a no-smoking sign in a prominent place at each entrance that:

- is the equivalent of A5 in area;

- displays the international no-smoking symbol in colour, is a minimum of 70mm in diameter; and

- carries the following words in characters that can be easily read, saying, 'No smoking. It is against the law to smoke in these premises'.

There are only a few exceptions to the regulations, but these include private dwellings, accommodation for guests and members (in designated bedrooms), off-shore installations and research and testing facilities. Specialist tobacconists are also exempt for the time that they are used for personal sampling of cigars and pipe tobacco (if certain conditions are met) and also for performers where the artistic integrity of a performance makes it appropriate for a person to smoke.

Asbestos

Historically asbestos was widely used in the UK, for example, as lagging on plant and pipe work and in insulation products such as fire-proofing panels. All types of asbestos can be dangerous if disturbed but the danger only arises when asbestos fibres become airborne and are breathed in. Exposure can cause such diseases as lung cancer, asbestosis and mesothelioma. Compensation claims can be brought as a result of an employer negligently exposing his employees to asbestos.

Claims have also successfully been brought by the wives of workers who were coming into regular contact with asbestos who brought the fibres home on their clothes. The wives then inhaled the fibres from the clothes whilst washing them and contracted asbestos-related conditions.

The Control of Asbestos Regulations 2012 ('the Asbestos Regulations') came into force on 6 April 2012. They revoke and replace, mostly by re-enactment, the Control of Asbestos Regulations 2006, which themselves brought together three sets of previous regulations which covered the prohibition of asbestos, the control of asbestos at work and asbestos licensing. The regulations require mandatory training for anyone liable to be exposed to asbestos fibres at work which includes maintenance workers and others who may come into contact or who may disturb asbestos, as well as those involved in asbestos removal work

If you are responsible for the maintenance and repair of your work premises, you must find out if there is any asbestos and where it is.

The Asbestos Regulations apply to all non-domestic premises and state that there is a duty on all those who have responsibility for the maintenance and/or repair of non-domestic premises to do all of the following. This duty could extend to lenders, investors, developers and companies acquiring other businesses – all of whom should be vigilant to avoid inheriting asbestos liabilities.

- Ensure that a suitable and sufficient risk assessment is carried out as to whether asbestos is or is liable to be present in the premises, taking into account building plans or other relevant information including the age of the premises.

- Ensure that an inspection is made of the parts of the premises which are reasonably accessible.

- Where the risk assessment shows that asbestos is or is liable to be present, the duty holder must ensure that a written plan is prepared identifying those parts of the premises concerned and specifying the measures which are to be taken for managing the risk.

- Provide information about their location and condition to anyone who is likely to work on or disturb such materials. This includes the emergency services.

Anyone carrying out work on asbestos installation, asbestos coating or asbestos insulating board (AIB) needs a licence issued by the Health and Safety Executive (HSE). It is clear that the HSE will enforce the Asbestos Regulations strictly and will be looking to impose large fines. Specialist advice should be sought if your work involves you coming into regular contact with asbestos.

The Mesothelioma Act 2014 (as amended by Diffuse Mesothelioma Payment Scheme (Amendment) Regulations 2015 and the Mesothelioma Lump Sum Payments (Conditions and Amounts) (Amendment) Regulations 2015) came into force on the 30 January 2014. It provides a method for mesothelioma sufferers who cannot bring a claim against their former employer (or their insurers) for whatever reason, to claim compensation, assuming that they were exposed to asbestos either negligently or as a result of a breach of statutory duty. The scheme pays a fixed amount based on the claimant's age. Employees will be eligible as long as they were diagnosed as suffering from mesothelioma on or after 25 July 2012.

3.6 Workers away from base

A substantial number of people work away from normal base operations. These include home and lone workers.

Home workers are those people employed to work at home for an employer and lone workers are those who are working away from the main work premises. Office cleaners, insurance salesmen, servers in coffee kiosks and home helps are a few examples.

This chapter also specifically deals with the special requirements of expectant mothers or those with infants. In addition, you should refer to the section on violence and consider whether other sections, particularly the sections on VDUs, stress and working time, also apply.

Legal requirements

Every business owner has a legal responsibility to protect the health and safety of their workforce. This includes staff who work on their own, either at the business premises or at some other location. Most of the regulations therefore apply to home or lone workers as well as to employees working at an employer's workplace.

Importantly, under the Management of Health and Safety at Work Regulations 1999, employers are also required to undertake a risk assessment of the work activities carried out by home workers.

The Occupier's Liability Acts of 1957 impose a duty on occupiers of the premises to take care of visitors in respect of dangers due to the state of the premises or things done or omitted to be done to it.

In addition, the Trade Union Reform and Employment Rights Act 1993 allows employees, including home workers, to stop working in the event of serious or imminent danger arising from the work that they are doing, without this affecting their employment rights.

Home workers, like other employees, have a duty to report all faults which may be a hazard to their own or other people's health and safety.

The Reporting of Injuries, Diseases and Dangerous Occurrence Regulations 2013 (RIDDOR) apply equally to home or lone workers (see chapter 4, section 1).

Risk assessment

Look for hazards

It may be necessary for employers to visit home workers to carry out a risk assessment. Home workers can help in identifying the hazards for their employers. In particular, consider the following:

- Do your employees have any medical condition that could compromise their health or safety?

- Could there be undue pressure caused by the work?

- Are you supplying specialist equipment for home workers?

- Is there any danger to other members of the family?

- Does any machinery need an electrical supply? If so, the business owner (not the manufacturer) is responsible for its safety. However, the safety of the electrical supply in the home (e.g. wall sockets) is the responsibility of the homeowner.

- Are any hazardous substances or chemicals being used?

- Does the work involve handling heavy loads?

- Special care must be given to expectant mothers and those with infants. The law requires that employers take account of the special circumstances of mothers-to-be and mothers who are breast-feeding or who have infants younger than six months. The employer should be aware that any risks affecting the mother would also include the child.

- Is there a danger of violence to those working alone? (See section 7 on violence.)

Decide who may be harmed and how

This may include home workers and members of their household, including children or visitors.

Reduce the risk of injury

- To avoid undue pressure, set reasonable limits on the amount of work that should be done in a period of time. Workers need to be trained. Also ensure that they are in regular contact wherever possible. Mobile phones could be encouraged and, if necessary, supplied. It may be useful to supply guidelines that may be followed in an emergency, listing contact names and useful telephone numbers.

- If equipment has been supplied, provide written instructions on how the equipment must be used and stored at the end of each day. Also:

  - ensure that the equipment is correct for the job;

  - provide the correct information and training;

  - check that the equipment is regularly maintained (and repair it when necessary);

  - ensure that the necessary personal protective equipment is provided (e.g. gloves when working with needles);

  - check that the plugs are not damaged and are correctly wired and maintained;

  - repair electrical equipment which may cause harm or injury;

  - check that there are no trailing wires and if there are any, tuck them out of the way (e.g. under a desk or table to prevent accidents).

- If hazardous substances or chemicals are being used, these should be identified with a black and orange label on the container. You must also provide the home worker with a set of instructions on how to handle the substance.

  Here is a checklist of things to be aware of when using substances, materials or chemicals that may be hazardous to health and safety (see also section 5 on hazardous substances):

  1. Are they flammable, toxic or corrosive?

2. Are they stored safely (e.g. could children reach them easily?).

3. Does anyone suffer from skin rashes, irritation, dizzy spells and sickness or have headaches when coming into contact with the chemical?

4. Does anyone suffer from asthma?

Do note that employers are only responsible for the substances and materials they provide to their home workers.

• Recommend work break periods and inform the home worker that other members of the family, who are unskilled and inexperienced, must not become involved with the work.

• If the work involves lifting heavy loads, the necessary lifting aids should be provided (see section 2 on manual handling).

• It is important for workers using VDUs to adjust the workstation to a comfortable position and take regular breaks from work. VDUs need to be placed in a position where lighting will not cause reflection or a glare on the screen. VDU users can request an eye examination and eye test from their employer. (For more information, see section 3 on upper limb disorders and section 4 on VDUs.)

• Under the Health and Safety (First Aid) Regulations 1981, you must ensure that adequate first aid provision is supplied for home workers. The exact provisions depend on the nature of the work activity and the risks involved.

Other points to note

HSE inspectors have the right to visit home workers. They can also investigate and help settle complaints about working conditions that could affect the health, safety or welfare of all employees, including home or lone workers.

3.7 Violence at work

Violence can consist of any verbal abuse or physical threat upwards. It may be between employees or, more likely perhaps, come from members of the public, depending on the nature of the business.

Legal requirements

The employer is under the usual general duty under the Health and Safety at Work Act 1974 (the HSW Act) to ensure, so far as is reasonably practicable, that the health safety and welfare of his employees is protected at work. Where there is a risk to employees (and in some cases, persons not in his employment) of physical violence in particular, as with a jeweller's shop or a 24-hour service supermarket, an employer must be particularly aware of his duties under the Management of Health and Safety at Work Regulations 1999, particularly with regard to risk assessments.

Certain businesses may need a clearly defined policy on violence at work. Such a policy, although relatively short, should be incorporated as a subsection to the statement of the health and safety policy.

Risk assessment

Look for hazards

An obvious example of an area where there may be a risk of violence would be when employees have to meet customers on their own, particularly if this is away from the usual workplace. When looking at whether there is a risk, it is very important in this area for employers to speak to their employees. Individual employees may have suffered some incidents of verbal abuse for example, which they may not have reported. When everyone's experience is considered, there may be more of a problem than it first appeared. You also need to think about what might have happened in a given situation if the violence had escalated. Any problems encountered by other similar businesses should also be considered.

Also consider the risk to members of the public. In one case, Mr M was stabbed in the back by a bouncer employed by the defendant, a nightclub owner, and, as a result, was left a paraplegic. The stabbing took place following an altercation earlier in the evening at the nightclub. At the close of the evening the bouncer went home, got a knife and returned, whereupon he met up with Mr M. In deciding whether or not the employer was responsible for his employee's conduct, the court considered the closeness of the connection between the act of the employee and the duties he was engaged to perform. In this case, it was stressed that if the job required an employee to use violence, then an act of violence will be more likely to be found to be linked to the employment. The employer was therefore responsible for Mr M's injuries.

Reduce the risk of injury

Measures to avoid or reduce the risk include reviewing an employee's training. Are they trained to spot the risk? Can they tell quickly if a customer is becoming angry and have they been trained to deal with this? Do they know of any emergency procedures, for example, the use of a panic button? Is there a policy for dealing with complaints and difficult customers? Where are customers seen? Is it possible to ensure that two employees are present at all times? If not, are there surveillance cameras and is someone always within call?

Consider whether there is sufficient space between the employee and the customer. Screens may be advisable but in some circumstances these can exacerbate the problem by the atmosphere they can create.

Are any valuables locked away out of sight where possible? Are there time-delay operated safes?

Particular risks are posed by employees visiting customers outside the workplace. If this is unavoidable, consider whether two employees should go or at least deliberate the extent to which a customer should be 'vetted' beforehand. Do ensure that the employee leaves clear information about where he is going and for how long, and has a means of calling for help quickly if necessary, for example, via a mobile phone. Consider personal alarms for high-risk staff.

Do not overlook risks posed by travel, particularly by those travelling late at night. Do consider providing safe transport home and do ensure that all areas outside the workplace are well lit.

If an incident does occur, this should prompt a thorough review of the measures in place. Also ensure that any affected employees are well supported following such an incident. In serious cases, a victim support scheme may help. The local police station will know where the nearest scheme is.

3.8 **Stress**

Stress, a reaction to undue pressure, can lead to mental and physical ill-health. It is uncertain whether stress at work is actually increasing or just appears to be, but it is definitely the case that employees are more aware that they may have a claim against their employer as a result. Insurers are certainly encouraging their insured to immediately notify them of any claim where stress, bullying, harassment or discrimination is alleged.

With the benefit of hindsight, it seems many stress claims could have been avoided by improved personnel procedures and communications, and by creating a more open and helpful culture in the workplace.

Legal requirements

The Court of Appeal gave comprehensive guidance in this area in February 2002 in the case of Sutherland v Hatton. Their guidelines included some practical advice for the employer as follows:

- Is psychiatric harm to any particular employee reasonably foreseeable?

- An employer is expected to know things that he ought reasonably to have known about a particular employee, but an employer can assume that an employee can withstand the normal pressures of the job unless he knows that the employee has a particular problem or vulnerability.

- The same test applies to each employee, whatever their job.

- The employer should consider the nature and extent of the work done by the employee and signs from the employee of impending harm to health. Such signs must be plain enough for any reasonable employer to realise that he should do something about it.

- The employer is usually entitled to take what he is told by the employee at face value, unless he has good reason to think that what he is told is incorrect.

- The employer is only expected to take steps that are reasonable in the circumstances. The court will take into account the size, resources and demands on the employer's business.

- The employer is only expected to take steps that are likely to be effective.

- An employer who offers a confidential advice service, with referral to appropriate counselling or treatment services, is unlikely to be found liable to his employee (but see below).

- The employer is not liable for allowing a willing employee to continue in the job if the only reasonable and effective step would have been to dismiss or demote the employee.

If it is possible to provide a confidential advice service with referral for counselling or treatment services, this would be seen by the Court as a significant factor. For example, providing the use of various stress telephone services (see the Appendices for the contact details for BUPA and the Centre for Stress Management who provide this facility). To be fair, this may well be beyond the scope of many small businesses and may not be required in any event. However, even the provision of such a service does not remove the need for an employer to consider the risk and take other effective action if it is indicated. Subsequent case law since Sutherland v Hatton has also confirmed that the provision of such services is not a 'panacea' by which employers can discharge their duty of care in all cases.

Ideally, the employer should be aiming to prevent stress from becoming a problem in the first place, but work-related stress is challenging to manage. Without always being able to determine the real source of stress, it is extremely difficult for employers to introduce stress management processes into the workplace. Careful risk assessments are therefore vital. The HSE has produced Management Standards and guidelines on work-related stress for employers and employees and their representatives (available at www.hse.gov.uk/stress)

There is also a specific area of law which deals with harassment, but we do not intend to deal with this in any detail in this book, so specialist advice should be sought. Careful consideration will need to be given to case law and issues deriving from the Protection from Harassment Act 1997. More information on this topic can also be found in Lawpack's book *Employment Law Made Easy* (www.lawpack.co.uk).

Risk assessment

Look for hazards

The usual risk assessment rules apply. Consider firstly whether there may be a problem. For example:

- Do your employees have poor sickness records?

- Are illnesses reported that may be stress-related (this covers a multitude of illnesses from a headache to irritable bowel syndrome and many others)?

- Is there a high staff turnover, poor time keeping and unhappiness among the employees or customers?

- Can any stress factors be identified? Talk to the staff.

- Is bullying and harassment sufficiently discouraged?

- Is there a culture of long hours, lack of communication and blame when things go wrong?

- Is there too much work for the number of staff? Look for pressures that could cause high and continuing levels of stress.

Then consider who may be harmed by any stress factors you may have found and what is reasonably practicable to do about it. Even if there are no obvious stress factors, it is worthwhile reviewing possible preventive measures.

Reduce the risk of injury

Preventive action may include:

- Encouraging an open and understanding culture.

- Ensuring good communications.

- Being understanding if employees admit to being under too much pressure.

- Ensuring that employees are properly trained for their work.

- Ensuring that employees have sufficient support.

- Allowing employees as much control as possible over their work and working conditions.

- Ensuring that employees are treated fairly.

- Preventing bullying and harassment by replacing line managers if necessary.

- Preventing bullying and harassment.

- Regularly monitoring the workforce for possible signs of stress.

- Providing a confidential advice service.

Action if there is a problem with workplace stress may include:

- Trying to address the sources of stress.

- Reviewing the preventive measures above and how effective they are for all employees. Also drawing up a further action plan, if necessary.

- Discussing with the employee concerned and trying to involve him in decisions.

- Considering whether the employee should be moved or work fewer hours, or otherwise varying his work. If he is off sick, keeping in touch. Beware of the employment law implications of changing the terms of an employee's contract or dismissing him.

- If necessary, enabling and encouraging the employee to seek further help through their doctor or a counselling service.

3.9 **Noise**

Noise at work can cause damage to hearing and high levels can cause deafness. It can also cause tinnitus (irritating ringing in the ear), communication difficulties and stress.

It is estimated that 3.5 per cent of the working population in the UK are now employed in call centres. Here, acoustic shock/trauma – the result of sudden, specific loud noises coming over the telephone headset – is emerging as a new cause for claims. This can cause hearing loss, dizziness and headaches.

However, as with work-related stress, it is extremely difficult to quantify the risks to your employees, as people have different sensitivities to noise.

Exposure to noise may affect hearing in three ways:

- **Temporary threshold shift:** this is a short-term effect, is reversible and depends to some extent upon an individual's susceptibility.

- **Permanent threshold shift:** recovery will take place but not fully, and only after the end of the exposure.

- **Acoustic shock/trauma:** as mentioned above, this involves sudden aural damages resulting from short-term intense exposure or one single exposure, for example, fireworks or major explosions.

It is vital, therefore, for employers to monitor carefully and control the exposure of all employees to noise from work activities.

Legal requirements

The Control of Noise at Work Regulations 2005 came into force on 6 April 2006, except for the music and entertainment sectors which came into force on 6 April 2008. Until then, the Noise at Work Regulations 1989 applied.

Daily personal noise exposure

The average amount of noise exposure during the whole working day is called 'the daily personal noise exposure'. The regulations also refer to the maximum noise (peak sound pressure) to which workers are exposed in a working day.

Noise is measured in decibels (dB). An 'A-weighting', sometimes written as 'dB(A)', is used to measure average noise levels and a 'C-weighting', or 'dB(C)', is used to measure peak, impact or explosive noises.

The regulations require you to take specific action at certain action values. These are:

- Lower exposure action values:
  - daily or weekly exposure of 80 dB

- peak sound pressure of 135 dB

- Upper exposure action values:
  - daily or weekly exposure of 85 dB
  - peak sound pressure of 137 dB

You are required to:

- Make hearing protection readily available to those that want it if noise exposure is between the lower and upper exposure action values.

- When the noise exposure exceeds the upper exposure action values, provide your workers with hearing protection and make sure that they use it property and it is maintained.

- Provide workers with training and information on hearing protection.

- Mark zones where noise exposure exceeds the upper exposure action value, with recognised signs to restrict entry.

- You must provide health surveillance (hearing checks) for all your workers who are likely to be regularly exposed above the upper exposure action value or are at risk for any reason.

There are levels of noise exposure which must not be exceeded (taking into account any reduction in exposure provided by hearing protection). These are:

- Daily or weekly exposure of 87 dB

- Peak sound pressure of 140 dB

Risk assessment

Look for hazards

If noise is an issue in the workplace, then the regulations require that every employer should ensure that a competent person makes a noise assessment.

The best way of assessing noise levels is employing someone with the necessary skill and experience to measure noise. See the Appendices for the contact details of the Association of Noise Consultants.

Reduce the risk of injury

- The regulations stress that if there is any likelihood of any damage, ear defenders or plugs ought to be provided.

- Ensure that any equipment provided to reduce noise exposure is actually used by employees.

- Choose the quietest equipment. It may provide useful to get some help from an independent consultant or the suppliers of new machinery. In one case, a policewoman was awarded substantial damages when she developed tinnitus caused by excessive noise, generated by a receiver during surveillance work for the Serious and Organised Crime Squad. If the defendant had addressed the problem of noise exposure, it would have been comparatively simple to provide an earpiece with a limited output and an on-off switch.

- Reduce the time that employees are exposed. Hearing damage is cumulative and depends not just on the noise levels, but on how long people are exposed to them.

- Put noisy machines in separate rooms.

- Fit silencers to equipment.

- Proper and regular maintenance of machinery is essential. It can deteriorate with age and become very noisy.

- Use sound insulation materials where possible.

- Provide hearing tests for those identified as being at risk.

- Employees are also under an obligation to use noise control equipment if provided. Once provided with ear protectors, employees must keep them in a sensible place and if there is any problem with them, they should draw their employer's attention to their difficulties.

For more information, obtain the HSE leaflet 'Noise at Work' (INDG362 rev 2).

3.10 Vibration

Vibration is often associated with noise (see the previous section).

Vibration is difficult to measure but excessive exposure can lead to either 'hand-arm vibration syndrome' (HAVS) or 'whole body vibration' (WBV). The former is a painful condition affecting blood circulation, nerves, muscles and bones in the hands and arms. It is caused by excessive use of hand-held power tools and machinery such as chipping hammers, grinders and chain saws. The latter is a condition that mainly affects drivers of heavy goods vehicles, tractors and dumpers; and can also cause low back pain and spinal injuries. See also section 3 on upper limb disorders as much of the information found there also applies.

Legal requirements

The Control of Vibration at Work Regulations 2005 came into force on 6 July 2005. They apply to both hand-arm and whole-body vibration. They provide a daily limit and weekly average exposure to the amount of vibration an employee may endure while working. They also require that the employer (who must eliminate vibration or reduce it to an amount as low as is practicable) must undertake a detailed risk assessment, health surveillance and provide information and training. The Provision and Use of Work Equipment Regulations 1998 (PUWER) and the Management of Health and Safety at Work Regulations 1999 also apply.

Risk assessment

Look for hazards

- The hazards are similar to those highlighted in the section on upper limb disorders.

- Employers should consider vibration levels when deciding what equipment or machinery to purchase.

- Are there any cases of vibration-related disorders in your workplace?

Reduce the risk of injury

- Efforts should be made when carrying out a job to limit the use of high vibration tools. Consider whether the process can be automated further.

- Tools should be checked regularly to minimise vibration and, if necessary, anti-vibration monitors should be fitted.

- Vary the work by alternating the different types of work and introducing job rotation.

- Provide training in skills, posture and warning symptoms to those at risk.

- Depending on the nature of the job, gloves can be used, although it should be emphasised that there are no gloves that can adequately protect people from vibration.

- When working with such machinery, it is important to have regular breaks. Workers can then keep their hands warm by massaging their fingers.

- Medical surveillance should be provided for those at risk.

- Ultimately, it is a matter of common sense that overuse of certain types of machinery will cause vibration, heat tingling and numbness in the hands.

3.11 **Electricity**

The principal hazards associated with the use of electricity are the risk of electrocution, burns, fire and explosions.

Each year, about 1,000 accidents at work involving shock and burns are reported to the HSE and about 30 of these are fatal. Fires can be started by anything, from poor electrical installation to explosions caused by static electricity igniting flammable vapours or dusts.

It is therefore fundamental to any business that all electrical equipment, wiring installations, meters and wires connected to them are maintained to the highest standard.

Regular checks and inspections are necessary, but how often these checks/inspections should be carried out will depend on the nature of the electrical equipment.

Legal requirements

The legal position is governed by the Electricity at Work Regulations 1989. Further guidance is given in the Memorandum of Guidance accompanying the regulations. This book can only give a brief overview of what is required. Briefly, Regulation 16 requires that no person shall be engaged in any work activity where technical knowledge or experience is necessary, in order to prevent exposure to danger or injury.

The regulations apply to all workplaces and cover all electrical equipment ranging from battery-operated equipment to high voltage installations.

Risk assessment

Shock

Electric shock results from an electric current flowing through the body. The effect can be fatal if the heart rhythm is disturbed for long enough so that it prevents blood flowing to the brain. Emergency action is vital in such cases. Resuscitation must be commenced quickly, firstly ensuring that there is no risk that the first aider will also suffer an electric shock.

Consider displaying a copy of the HSE's poster Electric Shock Action which shows what to do in an emergency.

Employers must prevent access to electrical danger. In one case, a 15 year-old claimant climbed over an eight foot steel fence into the defendant's electrical substation compound, ignoring clear signs warning him of the deadly risk he ran by entering. Once inside, he climbed up between the cooling fins and received an electrical shock from the overhead bars. The defendant was still held to be negligent for not providing a fence which efficiently protected the claimant.

Principal protective measures against electric shock are as follows:

- Protection against direct contact, i.e. by providing proper insulation for those parts of the equipment liable to be electrically charged.

- Protection against indirect contact, i.e. by providing effective earthing for metallic enclosures which are liable to be charged with electricity if the basic insulation fails for any reason.

- Fuses and circuit breakers should be of a type and rating appropriate to the circuit.

- Reduced voltage systems.

- Ensure that mains switches are easily accessible and clearly identified so that fuses and other devices are correctly rated for the circuit they protect.

- There must be a switch or isolator near each fixed machine to cut off power in an emergency.

- Enough socket outlets must be provided and all plug sockets and fittings must be sufficiently robust.

- Anyone carrying out electrical work must be competent to do so safely. If this means employing independent outside contractors, then do so.

- Cables, bulbs and other equipment must be replaced regularly and kept in good condition at all times. Suspect or faulty equipment should be taken out of use and labelled 'do not use'.

Appliances

- Any electrical appliances should be unplugged before cleaning or making adjustments. It is important to carry out regular checks and repairs, ideally by a qualified electrician. Even normal mains voltage (240 volts AC) can cause fatalities.

- Explosions can be caused by electrical apparatus or static electricity igniting inflammable vapours or dusts. Employers should ensure that waterproof or explosion protected equipment is supplied.

- The risks are greatest when electricity is used in harsh conditions, for example, portable equipment used outdoors.

- Reduce the voltage. Lighting can run at 12 or 25 volts and portable tools at 110 from an isolating transformer.

- Contact with overhead electric lines accounts for over half of the fatal electrical accidents each year. In circumstances where any equipment may come within nine metres of a power line, do not work under them without seeking advice from your electricity company.

Electricity can flash from overhead power lines even if the plant machinery and equipment is not touching them.

Fire

Clearly any outbreak of fire will be hazardous and it is crucial that employers have a structured, well-organised policy for preventing fires occurring. See chapter 2, section 3 for more information. However, this will include such practical considerations as:

1. Keeping the workplace tidy.

2. Ensuring that emergency routes are free from obstruction.

3. Designating competent persons who are responsible for ensuring that all plant machinery and equipment (that could potentially cause fire) is switched off every evening.

The local fire brigade will also be happy to advise on the necessary precautions.

Radiation

Electro-magnetic radiation ranges from radio waves at one end of the spectrum to ultraviolet light and gamma rays at the other.

Employers should endeavour to reduce exposure of their employees to all kinds of radiation. The complex issues involved in radiation cannot be dealt with in depth in this book, but it is important for employers to identify possible sources of radiation. If your employees will be exposed to radiation, you must refer to the Ionising Radiations Regulations 1999 which cover all work with ionising radiations, including exposure to naturally occurring radon gas.

All hazardous areas should also be marked and equipment should be maintained to minimise exposure. Employers should be advised of the need to wear protective equipment, for example, they should take care to avoid ultraviolet light by wearing suitable clothing and eye protection; if welding, special goggles or a face screen should be worn.

3.12 **Working at height**

Many industrial accidents occur when a ladder is used for a job when a tower scaffold or mobile access platform may have been safer and more efficient. Ladders are, of course, a common and useful means of access and are often used for short jobs. However, many ladder accidents happen during work lasting less than 30 minutes.

Legal requirements

The law in this area is governed by the Provision and Use of Work Equipment Regulations 1998 (PUWER), the Construction (Health and Safety Welfare) Regulations 1996 and the Construction (Design and Management) Regulations 2007 (as amended by the Construction (Design and Management) Regulations 2015) and the Work at Height Regulations 2005.

The Work at Height Regulations 2005 came into force on 6 April 2005. These abolished any qualification criteria for the necessary height that employees must be working at in order for there to be guidelines on safety. Now any work at height (including working at ground level over, for example, an excavation) requires safety procedures – such as guardrails – to be in place. Work with ladders must now be considered carefully and only undertaken if there is no other equipment that could otherwise be used; even then ladders should only be used for a short period of time while carrying out light work. These new regulations mean that formal training on how to work safely at heights must be given.

Risk assessment

The regulations place duties on employers and the self-employed, as well as those who have control over work at height, i.e. occupiers and business owners. You must make sure that all work is properly planned, supervised and carried out by people who are competent to do the job.

Within the risk assessment consider:

• Can working at height be avoided?

- Where it cannot be avoided work equipment or other measures should be used to prevent a fall.

- Where eliminating the risk of fall is not possible, work equipment or other measures should be used to minimise the distance and consequences of a fall should it occur.

Reduce the risk of injury

- Plan and organise properly all work at height.

- Take account of weather conditions that could endanger health and safety.

- Ensure those involved in working at heights are trained and competent.

- Ensure equipment is checked regularly.

- Check any risk from fragile surfaces that may be worked on.

- Check any risk from falling objects.

3.13 **Machinery**

The dangers of machinery and the number of accidents caused by dangerous machinery cannot be over-emphasised. Many cases involve young or inexperienced workers, where accidents could have been avoided through proper training.

The technical aspects of assessing and removing the risks of dangerous machinery is a vast subject and can only be dealt with briefly in this book. There are multiple standards, both national and international, which should be used for guidance.

Legal requirements

The HSE prosecutes cases involving serious personal injury caused by machinery on a daily basis. These can result in hefty fines. In July 2011, the manufacturer and operator of a computer-controlled conveyor system were fined a total of £115,000 when a worker was dragged through part of the conveyor system, after his clothes got caught while peering into a space to check a line of work.

The law in this area is largely contained in the Provision and Use of Work Equipment Regulations 1998 (PUWER).

Work equipment means any machinery, appliance, apparatus or tool, in addition to any assembly of components. The courts have tended to interpret this definition very widely. It could therefore include an electric drill, ladder, tractor, power press, paving slab or even a ship. PUWER states that every employer should do the following:

- Ensure that work equipment is constructed or adapted to be suitable for the purpose for which it is provided.

- Ensure that work equipment is maintained in an efficient state, in good working order and in good repair.

- Pay attention to specific risks created by the work equipment.

- Provide health and safety information, training and written instructions.

- Ensure that specific measures are taken to prevent risks arising from dangerous parts of the machinery (e.g. guards).

- Ensure that employees are not exposed to specific hazards, such as work equipment overheating.

Lifting operations

Under the Lifting Operations and Lifting Equipment Regulations (LOLER) 1998, lifting equipment or machinery provided for work should be:

- Strong and safe enough for its use.

- Marked with its safe working load.

- Installed and positioned to minimise risks.

- Used safely.

- Thoroughly examined and inspected by a competent person on an ongoing basis.

All equipment used at work for lifting and lowering loads, including attachments and accessories (except escalators), is covered by the regulations.

Risk assessment

Look for hazards

In any assessment of machinery, two factors must be considered:

- The mechanical factors, for example, design, reliability and safety devices.
- The human factors with regard to the physical operation of the machinery.

Mechanical factors

The types of hazards presented by machinery are described in detail in the British Standards and in other publications dealing with machinery safety. If the hazard could present a reasonably foreseeable risk to a person, the part of the machinery generating the hazard becomes a 'dangerous part'.

Any assessment must cover, not only the machinery and its customary operational mode, but also the maintenance, regular cleaning and care of the machine. Think about the following:

- **Traps in machinery:** if unguarded, machinery can cause a wide range of major injury accidents including hand, arm and finger amputations.
- **Entanglement hazards:** the risk of entanglement of hair, clothing or limbs is present whenever unguarded rotating parts, drills or chucks operate.
- **Contact hazards:** for example, hot surfaces, moving conveyor belts or rough surfaces.
- **Ejection hazards:** for example, metal particles, or sparks into the face or eyes.

The human factors

Think about the physical operation of the machinery, the systems of work, the potential for operator error, the routine maintenance procedures and the removal of waste. In addition:

- do not position the machine where customers or visitors may go;

- consider whether new starters or those who have changed their jobs may use the machine;

- note that workers can act foolishly, carelessly or make mistakes.

Reduce the risk of injury

There are various specific requirements for guards and other protection devices – too many to mention here. BSI's code of practice entitled *Guidance on safe use of machinery* (PD 5304:2005) is the authoritative guidance on machinery safety in the UK and is revised at regular intervals.

Briefly, it is fundamental that guards must be in place enclosing every dangerous part of the machine, as far as is practical. If it is not practical, another method should be explored, including interlocking the guards of the machine so that the machine cannot start before the guard is closed and it cannot be opened whilst the machine is working.

Also consider trip devices, overrun devices, mechanical restraints and two-hand control devices that require both hands to operate the machinery.

Extra training may be required for machine operators. Machines should all be checked after any modifications are made. The machine controls should be clearly marked to indicate what they can do and clearly marked emergency stop controls should be provided where necessary.

There are certain practical considerations that should be observed every time a person operates a machine or a potentially dangerous one. These may be listed on a checklist next to the machinery, for example:

- You must wear the appropriate protective clothing and equipment (e.g. safety glasses).

- You must know how to stop the machine before you start it.

- You must not use a machine unless you are authorised and trained to do so.

- All guards should be in position and all protective devices should be working.

- You must not endeavour to clean a machine that is in motion. Before cleaning, machines should be switched off and detached from any mains device.

- You must report any machine to the employer or supervisor if it is not functioning properly, or if there is a suggestion that it may be faulty in any way.

Maintenance

Compliance with the law requires the operation of planned maintenance programmes. These should incorporate records which identify each item of work equipment by serial number, the procedure to be undertaken, the frequency of maintenance and the individual responsible for undertaking the procedure.

3.14 **Construction**

In March 2013, HSE Inspectors visited 2,363 construction sites across Great Britain. A total of 631 enforcement notices were issued at 433 sites and inspectors gave orders for work to be stopped immediately in 451 instances.

The construction industry covers a wide field of operations from a large civil engineering project such as an office block to a self-employed tradesman carrying out minor repairs to a building.

Anyone working full-time in construction must consult a more detailed source of information. However, most offices and businesses require internal and external work at some stage. The extensive employment of casual labour and the real problems that can arise when contractors are working on an existing site contribute to the high incidence of accidents in the industry.

Scaffolding and roofing work is inherently dangerous. However, other potential risks include falling cables, inadequate work platforms and faulty and unstable equipment. Ill-health can also result from exposure to dust including asbestos, which can cause respiratory diseases and cancer. In addition, hernias and foot, hand and back injuries are all commonplace.

As a result, insurance premiums in this sector are soaring and those in the construction industry often find it difficult to get insurance. In breach of legal requirements, some firms trade without employer's liability insurance, which can attract fines of over £2,500 per day. A good safety record will assist a small to medium-sized enterprise in obtaining a competitive premium.

However, the risks associated with building sites do not just apply to builders. All business owners are legally required to ensure the safety of contractors whilst working on their premises.

Legal requirements

Under criminal law (the HSW Act), there is concurrent responsibility for the safety of operations. Therefore the company, which is the occupier of the premises or the site concerned, can be subject to prosecution if there are breaches of the law on its premises, even if they are caused by a contractor or subcontractor. The business owner must take every reasonably practicable measure to ensure compliance. In addition to the above, employers have duties under the following regulations:

- The Construction (Health, Safety and Welfare) Regulations 1996
- The Construction (Design and Management) Regulations 1994
- The Construction (Design and Management) Regulations 2007
- The Work at Height Regulations 2005

The Construction (Design and Management) Regulations 1994 (usually known as the CDM Regulations) were replaced on 6 April 2007. The 2007 Regulations also revoke and replace the Construction (Health, Safety and Welfare) Regulations 1996. The revised CDM Regulations apply to ongoing projects or projects after 6 April 2007. The Construction (Head Protection) Regulations 1989 were revoked from 6 April 2013 because it was felt they duplicated information about head protection contained within the later PPE at Work Regulations 1992.

If you are about to commission construction work as part of your business, you will have a responsibility to set certain standards on site and influence how the work is carried out without risks to the health and safety of the people working on the site. The CDM Regulations set out a number of key requirements and are supported by an Approved Code of Practice (ACoP) and several guidance notes. The regulations are very detailed and we would suggest that even if you are going to be involved in small, one-off projects, you obtain proper guidance.

People who are having work done on their own home, or on the home of a family member, that does not relate to their trade or business have no duties under the CDM Regulations 2007.

Someone who has duties under the CDM is called a 'duty holder'.

Duty holders

The duty holders, for the purposes of the CDM Regulations, remain the same as for the 1994 regulations. Duties are placed on:

- Commercial purchasers of construction/engineering works and services;
- Designers (anyone who prepares or modifies a design);
- Principal contractors (typically 'main' contractors);
- Contractors (typically sub-contractors); and
- CDM co-ordinators (formerly known as 'planning supervisors' under the 1994 regulations).

It is possible to carry out more than one role (e.g. design and build contractors could be the principal contractor, a contractor, a designer and the CDM co-ordinator).

Notifiable/non-notifiable projects

Some of the regulations' provisions are only triggered if the time the works are taking place on site is likely to involve more than 30 days or 500 person days of construction work (i.e it would take one person 500 days to complete). These projects are referred to as 'notifiable' and require that the local Health and Safety Executive (HSE) be notified of specific information relating to the project. You will need to refer to the regulations for the precise requirements. However, if a project has already been notified to the HSE under the CDM Regulations 1994, then there is no need to give a further notice under the 2007 regulations.

The 2007 CDM Regulations list duties that apply to all projects, and additional duties for notifiable projects. Despite similarities between the 1994 and 2007 CDM Regulations, 'duty holders' should now review their health and safety procedures. The HSE take the view that the later CDM Regulations reflect current best practice.

We recommend that you seek specialist advice on the scope and duties contained in the 2007 regulations if you are involved in construction work.

Risk assessment

Look for hazards and reduce the risk of injury

Hazards arise during even the most straightforward activities. For example, the risks associated with painting may include a risk of falling from a ladder and from inhalation of paints and solvents. Fitting out an office, on the other hand, may involve a risk of falling, electrical risks from portable equipment and exposure to asbestos.

Risk of falls

Check the following every time:

- Be especially aware of trespassers (to whom legal duties are also owed), particularly children.

- If the work is undertaken via a scaffold, platform or a ladder, it is vital to ensure that safe access onto, and off, the work area is facilitated with the proper equipment. This includes properly tied scaffolds, platforms which have guard rails and toe boards. Further guards such as brick guards may also be required to provide extra protection to prevent tools and materials from falling.

- Platforms, and any scaffolding, should be wide enough for the work to be done and they should be fully boarded. The boards themselves should be properly supported and should not overhang excessively.

- The scaffolding should be inspected regularly, at least once a week, and more regularly in inclement weather.

- For scaffolding, before starting work on any scaffold or other working platforms, an employer must follow some relatively obvious (but often ignored) safety precautions, to include the following:

  - Any equipment is installed by competent and specialist people.

  - A handover certificate is supplied by the provider of the equipment (to cover matters such as the operation and maintenance of equipment).

  - Any necessary barriers or covered walkways are provided.

  - Equipment is protected from the weather if necessary.

  - Appropriate notices are attached to warn not only employers or sub-contractors but also vandals or trespassers of the dangers of the equipment.

  - As far as roofs are concerned, there must be a safe means of moving across the roof and onto sloping and fragile roofs. Purpose-made roof ladders or crawling boards should be supplied.

- Home-made ladders should not be used under any circumstances and have been the cause of many industrial accidents.

- Broadly similar rules apply for tower scaffolds and mobile and suspended access equipment.

- As ever, the person responsible for the scaffold or the mobile access equipment should be fully trained and the work platforms should be provided with guard rails, toe boards and other suitable barriers. They should be on firm and level ground and there should be safe access to and from the platform.

- For towers and working platforms, follow the manufacturers' instructions. Do not exceed the maximum height allowed for a given base dimension.

- In cases where it is impracticable to provide a working platform, boatswain's chairs and seats can be used. Employers should also give consideration to using safety harnesses. Whilst a harness may not prevent a fall, it will minimise the risk of serious injury.

- Even in offices it must be possible for windows to be opened and cleaned safely. You may need to fit anchor points if window cleaners have to use harnesses.

Risks from machinery and powered hand tools

- You do not work from height unless it is essential.
- Only competently trained people should deal with any specialised equipment and training should be given in the use of such equipment, as required.
- The manufacturer's instructions should be observed at all times.

Risks from electrocution

- Other common, perhaps less obvious, problems on building sites are injuries from electricity cables, gas pipes, etc. In circumstances where digging work has to be undertaken, this should take place well away from any such cables and pipes, or cable detection devices should be used.
- Employers will be expected to consider service plans, safe digging practices and manufacturers' or suppliers' briefing documentation.
- Check that there are no overhead power lines in the way or any obstructions.

Risks from collapses of excavations

- Trench sites can collapse suddenly whatever the nature of the soil. Any excavations deeper than 1.2 metres must have the sides supported.
- Dig well away from the underground services.

3.15 **Vehicles in the workplace**

Many deaths and serious injuries that occur in the workplace involve the use of cars, vans, heavy goods vehicles, etc. The most common types of incident involve people being struck by a moving vehicle, people falling from a vehicle, objects falling from vehicles or from vehicles overturning. However, there is also a risk of accidents due to over-tiredness. Later in this section we deal with the legal requirements for tachographs.

Legal requirements

Vehicles can be included in the definition of 'work equipment' in the Provision and Use of Work Equipment Regulations 1998 (PUWER). The legal requirements for tachographs are contained in both UK domestic law and European legislation which also applies to England and Wales. The relevant European regulation is Regulation 3821/85ECC.

Risk assessment

Look for hazards

- Any vehicles used must be assessed regularly and new vehicles should be provided when appropriate.

- Look also at those who use the vehicles and the condition in which they use them: is there a risk of overheating or the employee working long hours and becoming sleepy? The fact that the greatest risk of being killed at work is due to occupational road use has long been recognised. Employers should therefore create systems for monitoring insurance claims, accident records and damage reports. If there is a problem, then the employer should take action.

- Consider the risks to employees during the repair and maintenance of vehicles, for example, back injuries are particularly commonplace. Also consider explosion risks when draining and repairing fuel tanks.

Reduce the risk of injury

Preventative steps or precautions can be taken to minimise the risk of accidents occurring.

The vehicles

- Are there any potentially dangerous parts on any vehicles, for example, exposed exhaust pipes?

- Have seat belts been fitted?

- Have the vehicles been serviced comprehensively and regularly?

- Is there a safe means of access to and from cabs, vans or heavy goods vehicles?

- Are the drivers carrying out basic safety checks before driving the vehicles?

- Are the vehicles provided with appropriate reflectors, horns, lights, etc?

Vehicle activities

- Are there pre-employment checks on drivers' licences and their fitness to drive?

- Drivers should be given full and comprehensive guidance as to how to reverse their vehicle and park it appropriately. Employers should ensure that there are external and side mounted mirrors to facilitate the best possible all-round visibility. Also consider whether a banksman should be provided to assist with any reversing procedure. This is particularly important for larger vehicles. Claims regularly involve crushing injuries to feet as a result of reversing vehicles.

- Employers should consider whether there is a designated parking area and advise that vehicles and any trailers are securely braked before being parked and subsequently locked.

- Proper guidance should also be given as to the loading and unloading of vehicles including the following:

- Check that the loading or unloading that is being carried out is done in an area that is even and free from obstruction.

- Loading and unloading should take place in a safe place away from traffic and pedestrians if possible.

- The load should be spread evenly to avoid the vehicle becoming unstable.

- Guidance should be given as to the capacity of any vehicle so that it is not overloaded.

- The load should be secured as far as possible.

- Consider using protective equipment to prevent, for example, the inhalation of asbestos dust from brake and clutch lining pads or to prevent contact with battery acid.

- Employers should clearly set out that mobile telephones should not be used while employees are driving and that smoking in work vehicles is prohibited.

The workplace

- Employers should ensure that the vehicle routes are appropriate for the size and number of vehicles that will use the route, i.e. that they are well maintained, free from hazard, even and of the proper width.

- Consider providing speed humps or barriers to reduce vehicle speeds and to keep vehicles and pedestrians apart.

- Traffic signs should be provided if appropriate, such as 'Give Way', 'No Entry' and any speed limit signals should also be erected.

- Adequate parking should be provided and pedestrian crossings should possibly be considered. Is a one-way system appropriate, for example?

- Systems should be in place to deal with breakdowns and other emergencies, such as the use of mobile phones and safe systems of work for working on or by roads.

Tachographs

All vehicles exceeding 3.5 tonnes used for carrying goods and passengers must be fitted with an EC approved tachograph to record the number of hours driven by the driver, in addition to his other work and rest periods.

Certain vehicles are exempt from the European rules but then the UK domestic rules apply. Further information can be obtained from your local Department for Transport testing station. Generally, however, the following should be noted:

- The daily driving limit is nine hours (which can be increased to ten hours twice a week) taken between two consecutive daily rest periods. After four and a half hours of cumulative or continuous driving, a driver must take a break of at least 45 minutes.

- Tachographs must be inspected at a Department for Transport approved tachograph calibration centre at the following times:

  - Every two years to check that the system is working properly.

  - Every six years to calibrate the tachograph.

- Drivers must carry their record charts (not photocopies) for the current week and for the last day of the previous week. Charts must be given to employers within 21 days.

- Employers must do the following:

  - Keep all charts for two years.

  - Make regular checks (weekly basis) to make sure that the rules are being obeyed.

  - Pass over record charts to enforcement authorities when so requested. Failure to do so is a criminal offence.

Fourth EU Motor Directive 2000/26/EC

This European Directive came into force on 20 January 2003. The aim of the Directive is to assist those people injured in a road traffic accident in other European countries to make a claim for compensation. This system will ensure that claimants will be able to pursue the claim quickly by being able to identify the insurer of the liable vehicle from its registration number.

Each country therefore has to set up an information centre to provide insurer information from the registration number. In the UK, this is the Motor Insurers' Bureau(MIB) in Milton Keynes – see the Appendices for their contact details. Requests must be made in writing by submitting a claim form together with any supporting documents. The MIB will then write to you or your representative to confirm that your claim has been received and will give you a reference to use in all future correspondence.

Every vehicle in circulation comes under the Directive. This does create difficulties in respect of vehicles insured on a fleet policy (where the insurer may not hold details of each vehicle) and also on motor trade policies (where there are rapid changes of ownership). Possible solutions may include a requirement on the policyholder to submit details regularly to their insurer or directly to the database.

3.16 **Farming**

Agriculture has one of the highest fatality rates of all industries, with almost one person a week being killed in the ten-year period finishing 2008/09. There were 29 reported fatalities in the 2012/13 year. Occupational risks include chemicals, potentially dangerous machinery and working at heights. Furthermore, agriculture is responsible for 15 to 20 per cent of workers' deaths in Great Britain each year. This is all the more alarming considering that 464,000 people work in agriculture, which represents only 1 per cent of the working population.

In 2012/13, about 3,800 agricultural and other related trade injuries were reported to HSE. As well as the obvious personal cost of injury, there is a sizeable financial one. Farming, combined with forestry and horticulture, loses about £190 million a year as a result of injuries. Musculoskeletal injuries are common, albeit decreasing, with 439,000 out of 1,073,000 workers suffering from them.

In short, agriculture continues to be the most hazardous industry to work in. Anyone involved in farming should seek separate detailed advice. Many of the previous regulations referred to apply and you should also refer to the previous relevant sections, including: section 1, Slips/trips; section 2, Manual handling; section 5, Hazardous substances; section 6, Workers away from base; section 8, Stress; section 9, Noise; section 10, Vibration; section 11,

Electricity; section 13, Machinery; and section 15, Vehicles in the workplace. In addition, specific regulations relating to agricultural businesses will apply.

Further information can be obtained from the agricultural section of the HSE website; in particular, 'Farmwise', which forms the basis of agricultural health and safety advice.

CHAPTER 4

Accidents at work

Even the company which follows the health and safety law to the letter will experience an accident in the workplace at some time or other. It may only be a secretary with a paper cut requiring a plaster or a bruise following a trip down a staircase, but when injuries and accidents occur, you must be able to deal with them. If an incident does occur, then you should follow the checklist below.

4.1 Checklist

Take the action required to deal with the immediate risk

If first aid is required, ensure that the first aid box is replenished.

Complete the accident book

This should be completed for all accidents at work.

RIDDOR forms

The Reporting of Injuries, Diseases and Dangerous Occurrences Regulations 2013 (RIDDOR) revoked the RIDDOR Regulations 1995 and came into force on 1 October 2013. The 2013 Regulations require employers, the self-employed or those in control of workplaces to report some work-related accidents, diseases and dangerous occurrences to the

Health and Safety Executive (HSE). Since 12 September 2011, only fatal and major injuries/incidents can be reported by phone. All other work-related injuries/incidents, which fall under RIDDOR, have to be reported via one of seven online forms available on the HSE's website at www.hse.gov.uk/riddor/report.htm.

Which accidents must I report?

The 2013 Regulations have amended the list of accidents that need to be reported.

- **Death or major injury:** if an employee, self-employed person or person working on your premises is killed or suffers a major injury, or a member of the public is killed in an accident connected with work, you must notify the HSE immediately. You must also notify immediately where something happens like a fire or explosion which stops work for more than 24 hours. Within ten days, you must follow this up by completing online accident form F2508 Report of an Injury – see sample on page 112.

- **Specified injuries to workers:** The list of specified injuries in RIDDOR 2013 has replaced the previous list of major injuries in RIDDOR 1995. A specified injury must be reported. The injuries classed as specified injuries are as follows:
  - Fractures, other than to fingers, thumbs and toes
  - Amputations
  - Any injury likely to lead to permanent loss of sight or reduction in sight
  - Any crush injury to the head or torso causing damage to the brain or internal organs
  - Serious burns (including scalding) which covers more than 10% of the body or causes significant damage to the eyes, respiratory system or other vital organs
  - Any scalping requiring hospital treatment
  - Any loss of consciousness caused by head injury or asphyxia
  - Any other injury arising from working in an enclosed space which leads to hypothermia or heat-induced illness or requires resuscitation or admittance to hospital for more than 24 hours

- **Over seven-day injury:** as from 1 April 2012, if an accident connected with work results in an employee or a self-employed person working on your premises having seven days away from work or being unable to do the full range of duties, then online form F2508 Report of an Injury must be completed within 15 days. The form will ask you to specify the relevant authority to whom the incident should be reported (see chapter 1). Before 1 April 2012, there was a requirement to report injuries resulting in an absence of over three days. Employers and others with responsibilities under RIDDOR must still keep a record of all over three-day injuries – if the employer has to keep an accident book, then this record will be enough.

- **Non fatal accidents to non-workers:** These must be reported if they result in an injury and the person is taken directly from the scene of the accident to hospital for treatment to that injury. It should be noted that examinations and diagnostic tests do not constitute 'treatment' in such circumstances. There is also no requirement to report a situation where a person is taken to hospital as a precaution when no injury is apparent

- **Dangerous occurrences:** any dangerous occurrences must be reported using online form F2508 Report of a Dangerous Occurrence. Dangerous occurrences are 'near-miss events' that could have resulted in injury and include:

  - collapse, overturning or failure of load-bearing parts of lifts and lifting equipment;

  - explosion, collapse or bursting of any closed vessel or associated pipework;

  - failure of any freight container in any of its load-bearing parts;

  - accidental release of a biological agent likely to cause severe human illness.

  This list is not exhaustive and a full list of dangerous occurrences can be obtained from the HSE's website.

- **Disease:** if a doctor notifies you that an employee suffers from a reportable work-related disease, then you must complete online form F2508a Report of a Case of Disease and send it to the HSE within ten days. Again, the form will ask you to specify the relevant authority to whom the incident should be reported. Diseases include:

Completed example of RIDDOR form F2508 Report of an Injury

HSE

Health and Safety
Executive

Report of an injury

Note: this is a preview of your form and does NOT represent the submitted details of your notification, which will include the Notification number for reference

About you and your organisation

Notifier name	Miss Joanna Bloggs		
Job title	Sales Ledger Clerk		
Organisation name	Executive Park		
Address	Avalon Way, ANSTEY AB1 2CD		
Phone no	01234 56789	Fax Number	
Email Address	jb@ep.gb		

Where did the incident happen

The incident happened at the above address

About the incident

Incident Date	01/05/2014	Incident Time	10:37
In which local authority did the incident occur (Country, Geographical Area and Local Authority)?			
England, Avon, Bristol			
In which department or where on the premises did the incident happen?		Accounts	
What type of work was being carried out (generally the main business activity of the site)?			
Business services - Legal and accounting activities - Accounting, auditing; tax consltcy			

The enforcing authority for the address where the incident happened is the Local Authority

About the kind of accident

Kind of accident	Lifting and handling injuries
Work process involved	Storing/warehousing
Main factor involved	Lifting, carrying, standing up
What happened	Acute back pain caused by lifting heavy box of files

About the injured person

Injured persons name	Mr Fred Smith		
Injured persons address	Avalon Way, ANSTEY AB1 2CD		
Phone no			
What was their occupation or job title?	Office assistant		
Gender	Male	Age	23
Work Status	The injured person was one of my employees.		

About the injured person's injuries

Severity of the injury	Injury preventing the injured person from working for more than 7 days
Injuries	Part of the body affected

- certain poisonings
- occupational dermatitis
- skin cancer
- chrome ulcer
- occupational asthma
- pneumoconiosis
- asbestosis
- mesothelioma
- hepatitis
- anthrax
- tetanus
- hand/arm vibration syndrome

This list is not exhaustive and a full list of reportable diseases can be obtained from the HSE's website. (See the Appendices for a list of the most common occupational diseases and their causes.)

- **Gas incidents:** A distributor, filler, importer or supplier of flammable gas must report any death or major injury they learn of in connection with the gas they distributed, filled, imported or supplied. This must be reported using online form F2508G1.

  A gas engineer registered with the Gas Safe Register must report any gas appliances or fittings they consider to be dangerous to the extent that it may cause death or major injury. This can be due to the design, construction, installation, modification or servicing of the appliance or fitting. This must be reported using online form F2508G2.

Accident investigation

It is essential to ascertain the cause of an accident and, once the cause has been established, to prevent a recurrence of that accident. Consider whether you need to take witness statements and record other information for future use, for example, in case there may be a prosecution or a civil claim. See sections 4 and 5 for further information.

Find out what happened and why. Also look at near misses, as often it is only by chance that someone was not injured. Most accidents have more than one cause so try and deal with the root causes.

Post-accident risk assessment

This should be considered in any case and certainly undertaken in the case of a serious or recurring accident.

Tell your insurer

It will be a term of your policy that certain accidents must be reported. Check your own employer's liability insurance policy for details. See also section 4 on defending a civil claim.

4.2 HSE investigations

As discussed in section 1.2, health and safety law is enforced by inspectors from the HSE or by local authority inspectors. They may visit at any time, not only after an accident at work, and they have the right to enter any workplace without having to give notice. Low-risk businesses such as shops or offices will no longer be subject to regular health and safety inspections by the HSE. However, compliance with health and safety legislation is still required.

The HSE now operates a Fee for Intervention (FFI) cost recovery scheme, which came into effect on 1 October 2012. Under The Health and Safety (Fees) Regulations 2012, those who break health and safety laws are liable for recovery of HSE's related costs, including inspection, investigation and taking enforcement action.

What will happen if the inspector finds a breach?

The action taken by the inspector will depend upon the nature of the breach. He may deal with the matter in the following ways:

Informally

If the breach is minor, he may simply tell the employer how to comply with the law and explain why it is necessary.

An improvement notice

If the breach is more serious, an improvement notice may be issued. This tells the employer to do something positive in order to comply with the law. After serving the notice, the inspector will discuss with the employer what needs to be done, why and when. This will also be outlined in the notice.

The notice also outlines the period within which to undertake the action. It must be at least 21 days. An inspector can take further legal action if the notice is not complied with within the specified time period but the employer may also appeal to an industrial tribunal once the notice is served if they are not happy with it.

A prohibition notice

If an activity involves a risk of serious personal injury, a prohibition notice may be served prohibiting the activity immediately or after a specified period of time. Such a notice will direct that specified activities should not be carried out unless certain remedial measures have been complied with. It is served where there is an immediate threat to life and in anticipation of danger.

An employer may also appeal a prohibition notice. However, unlike an appeal against an improvement notice where the notice is automatically suspended, the requirements of the notice continue to apply. Appeals are dealt with by industrial tribunals. Contact should be made with your local HSE who will provide you with further information on appealing.

Prosecution

In some cases, a prosecution may be initiated. This can be against a company and/or an individual. This is frequently the outcome of an employer failing to comply with an improvement or prohibition notice but an inspector can also institute proceedings without serving a notice. Cases are normally heard in a Magistrates' Court but there is provision for a case to be heard in the Crown Court. Much depends upon the gravity of the offence. The court has considerable scope for punishing offenders and deterring others. In more serious cases, there are unlimited fines and, in some cases, prosecution can result in imprisonment.

However, the HSE are unlikely to prosecute for minor breaches of the law and will often give the employer the opportunity to explain the circumstances and give their views. The employer's attitude to health and safety and the safety record of the business in general are taken into account when they are deciding whether or not to prosecute. Particular factors, taken into account when deciding whether to prosecute, are set out in the HSE's Enforcement Policy Statement. This can be obtained from the HSE. For more detailed information regarding HSE prosecutions, please refer to section 4.5.

A local authority has the same power to prosecute as the HSE.

Corporate liability

A company is liable when it commits an offence which is proven to have been committed with the consent or connivance of the company or is attributable to the neglect on the part of a director, manager, secretary or other similar officer. Both the individual(s) involved as well as the company may be prosecuted and found guilty of an offence. See section 6 for further information. This means that a company director can be prosecuted even though the act or omission resulting in an offence was committed by a junior official or executive.

4.3 **How a civil claim works**

Despite concerns about a 'claims culture', a surprisingly small percentage of accidents leads to claims. However, it is helpful to understand the basic rules applicable to personal injury claims, whether you are a potential defendant or claimant.

Liability

For a personal injury claim to succeed, it must be proved that someone else was negligent or in breach of statutory duty, and that the negligence or breach caused the injuries and other losses. Negligence is careless conduct causing damage to others. As stated previously in Chapter 1, the question of whether a breach of duty gives rise to civil liability is something that needs careful consideration. The position has changed for accidents occurring after 1 October 2013 as a result of the introduction of the Enterprise and Regulatory Reform Act 2013.. Specialist legal advice should always be sought from a personal injury solicitor approved by the Law Society.

The claimant must show that the defendant owed a duty of care to the claimant. An employer clearly owes a duty of care to his employee. The claimant also has to establish that the defendant has not taken care of him and that the claimant has suffered damage as a result. A negligent act can be a positive action, or simply an omission to do something. If a claimant was also partly to blame for an accident ('contributorily negligent'), his damages will be reduced by the appropriate percentage.

Who can claim?

Someone who has suffered a physical injury can obviously claim. More technical rules govern claims for psychiatric injury, such as post-traumatic stress disorder (PTSD). The courts are concerned with not 'opening the floodgates' of PTSD claims and strict rules have accordingly been developed which limit, sometimes rather artificially, who may bring a claim for damages for PTSD.

If someone has died as a result of an accident or disease, the deceased's claim for damages for personal injuries and other losses may be pursued through his estate. Any dependants may have a claim for loss of support. A bereavement award, now £12,980 (post April 2013), may also be claimed by the deceased's spouse or a minor's parents (subject to some further limitations).

What can be claimed?

A claim is usually separated into general damages, special damages and future loss. Interest is payable as well.

- **General damages:** include damages for pain and suffering, i.e. compensation for the injury itself. This is often a surprisingly small proportion of a large award. The largest awards are usually made where there are substantial claims for loss of earnings or the cost of care – see below.

- **Special damages:** items of past loss which are capable of being calculated reasonably accurately. They include loss of earnings, travelling expenses for medical treatment, cost of medical treatment and medicines and personal effects damaged in an accident.

- **Future loss:** the calculations can be quite complex. Essentially, if there are losses that are likely to continue into the future, the claimant will not just recover the annual loss multiplied by the number of years for which the loss is likely to last. A multiplier is applied, which takes into account a discount to adjust for the fact that the claimant will be receiving the money all at once rather than over a period of years (and can therefore invest it and obtain interest on it) as well as for the other uncertainties of life.

- **Interest:** payable at different rates depending on the type of damages. Interest on special damages runs from the date of the accident, and interest on general damages runs only from the date of the service of proceedings.

- **Benefits:** received from the state by the claimant and may be deducted from the damages at the end of the case. The Compensation Recovery Unit (CRU) calculates the benefits received and supplies a certificate to the defendant (or more usually his insurers). The defendant then has to pay the CRU the amount demanded when the case is settled and will then pay the claimant's damages net of that deduction. Not all the benefits are necessarily deducted from the damages; complicated rules apply. Any charges incurred as a result of NHS treatment will also be collected by the CRU.

- **Provisional damages:** once a claim is settled, the claim has ended and no further claims can be brought. An exception to this rule is if provisional damages are awarded. This may occur if there is, at the time of settlement, a chance of significant future deterioration in the claimant's condition. A common example is when, following a head injury, there is a small increased risk of developing epilepsy. The claimant will be given the opportunity to make a further claim within a specified period should the deterioration occur.

How a claim can be made

It is important to consult a specialist solicitor who has Personal Injury Panel membership which is obtained by becoming accredited through the Law Society's Personal Injury Accreditation Scheme. Most solicitors will offer an initial free interview when the question of costs, as well as the likely merits of a claim, can be discussed. Citizens Advice Bureaux may provide initial advice and can also help with choosing a solicitor. The Law Society maintains a list of specialist solicitors (see the Appendices for their details).

Generally, the person who was negligent or their employers will be sued. In practice, the defendant's insurers deal with the defence of most personal injury claims. If injuries result from a criminal act, then a claim may be lodged with the Criminal Injuries Compensation Authority (see the Appendices for their contact details).

Most personal injury claims settle without the need for a court hearing. There are, however, built-in unavoidable delays in any personal injury claim. At least one medical report has to be obtained to prove the injuries. It may be necessary to wait some years before an accurate prognosis is available.

In the majority of cases involving a claim arising from an accident that occurred after 31 July 2013, the Pre-Action Protocol for Low Value Personal Injury (Employers Liability and Public Liability) Claims now applies at the outset. This Protocol requires information to be sent via an electronic portal. Strict time limits apply. The aim of this Protocol is to ensure that:

(1) the defendant pays damages and costs using the process set out in the Protocol without the need for the claimant to start proceedings;

(2) damages are paid within a reasonable time; and

(3) the claimant's legal representative receives the fixed costs at each appropriate stage.

Otherwise in cases where the sums claimed are valued in excess of £25,000 and for all cases which fall outside or exit this particular Protocol a typical case will pass through the following stages:

• **Pre-action protocol:** the parties exchange information before the proceedings are started. Normally the claimant's solicitor will send the defendant's insurers a detailed letter setting out the arguments on liability and giving a general idea of the value of the case. The defendant then has three months to respond. If the defendant then admits liability, there will be a further period of negotiation in an attempt to settle the claim.

- **Starting proceedings:** a claimant's statement of case will be served and the claimant must sign a Statement of Truth stating that the contents of the statement of case are true. If the statement of case is subsequently found to be untrue, then the claimant may be punished for contempt of court. The defendant must acknowledge the service of proceedings within 14 days, failing which the claimant may enter judgment.

- **Defence:** usually this must be served within 28 days at the latest from the service of proceedings. Extensions of time may be granted, but only if there is a good reason.

- **Allocation:** the court will decide which 'track' the case should be allocated to after the parties have filed an Directions Questionnaire. Generally, personal injury claims, where the damages for pain and suffering are probably worth less than £1,000, will be allocated to the Small Claims Track and will be dealt with more informally. (Very limited costs will also be awarded to the successful party, so it is unlikely to be economic to instruct a solicitor.) Claims worth over £1,000 but less than £25,000 will be allocated to the Fast Track (where trials are usually limited to one day), and claims over that amount to the Multi Track.

- **Disclosure:** exchange of lists between the parties of the documents relevant to the case. The lists have to be verified by a Statement of Truth. Parties have a duty to disclose all of the documents that may be relevant to a case, even if harmful to that party's own case (see page 124 for the types of documents which must be disclosed).

- **Exchange of witness statements and expert reports:** the court will set a timetable for this. The aim is that evidence should be disclosed in good time before any trial in order to avoid time wasting in court and to maximise the chance of a negotiated settlement.

- **Case management hearing:** this is more likely to happen in a Multi Track case. The aim of the hearing is for the judge and the parties, or their legal representatives, to review the case, to explore whether some matters can be agreed and to see whether it is possible to negotiate a settlement. Mediation may be considered and is actively encouraged by the courts.

- **Trial:** this is meant to be a last resort and the parties will have been encouraged to settle before this stage is reached. A Fast Track trial will normally last only one day and expert evidence is usually in writing. Multi Track trials may last many days depending on the complexity of the case. In both cases, a trial window will have been allocated earlier on in the case so the parties should have an idea of roughly when and where the case is likely to be heard. Depending on the case, a more accurate date is given nearer the time of trial. Being a witness can be very stressful – see the checklist in the next chapter for some helpful hints.

- **Payments/offers:** damages are usually paid by the defendant's insurer, subject to any excess applicable. In long running claims, interim payments may be obtained. These are payments on account of the eventual likely damages that may be awarded. Defendants may make an offer to settle, or a 'Part 36 offer', to try and make the claimant settle. If the claimant does not beat the amount offered at trial, he is likely to be ordered to pay the costs of both sides from the date of the payment made. A claimant may also make a Part 36 offer setting out what he would accept in settlement of his claim. A defendant who fails to beat such an offer will also be penalised in costs and will have to pay a penalty rate of interest as well.

- **Costs:** the defendant's insurer also usually pays these if the claimant is successful.

- **Limitation:** court proceedings in personal injury cases must generally be started within three years of the date of the accident. More time may be allowed, for example, if the claimant did not know of the injury at that time. In industrial disease cases, such as mesothelioma claims, claims are commonly brought many years after first exposure as the disease may only appear much later. The court also has the discretion to allow more time in some cases, but this should not be relied on if it can be avoided. Minors and people with a mental disability generally have longer. Different periods apply to different types of claims. Claimants should therefore seek legal advice as quickly as possible after they become aware of the possibility of a claim.

- **Inquests:** the purpose of an inquest is not to establish or apportion blame but to establish the cause of death. Coroners will generally prevent questions to witnesses if it appears that they are only trying to establish fault. Evidence is given on oath.

The Coroners and Justice Act 2009, which came into force in July 2013, provides significant new powers for coroners to compel witnesses to attend and produce documents as well as widening the circumstances in which a jury is required.

An inquest will be held when the coroner has reasonable cause to suspect that the deceased has died an unnatural or violent death or he has died a sudden death, the cause of which is unknown, or has died in prison. There will not be an inquest where serious criminal proceedings result from the death.

There may be a jury, for example, if the death was caused by an accident, disease or poisoning. Notice of these must be given to a government department or inspector under any Act. An inquest into a death may also be held with a jury if the senior coroner thinks that there is sufficient reason for doing so.

Interested parties have the right to question witnesses at the inquest either in person or through their legal representative.

Possible verdicts at an inquest include unlawful killing, natural causes, industrial disease, lack of care, suicide, accidental death, misadventure or an open verdict.

Whilst inquests can be helpful to the bereaved as a milestone which has been passed and possibly as the source of some explanation of what happened, they can also be extremely traumatic. This may be particularly the case as some coroners ask the pathologist to go through the whole postmortem report in horrifying and unnecessary detail. Normally the coroner's officer warns relatives in advance that they may wish to leave the court at this point, but this is not always the case.

Sources of further information

Citizens Advice Bureaux can give general advice. The Law Society can recommend suitably specialised solicitors. The latest version of the Civil Procedure Rules, together with useful links to other sources of information, can be found on the Ministry of Justice's website at www. justice.gov.uk/civil/procrules_fin (see the Appendices).

4.4 **Defending a civil claim**

For the way a claim works, see the previous section. This section covers additional matters specifically relevant to defendants. Generally, an employer will have an insurer who will deal with civil claims. Employer's liability cover is compulsory. However, the employer must co-operate fully with that insurer, in particular by promptly telling the insurer of any possible claim and quickly forwarding any correspondence or proceedings to the insurer. The employer must also be open with the insurer and tell him anything that may be relevant to the claim. If the employer does not, the insurer may be entitled to refuse to pay under the policy. The insurer may pay the claimant but may seek to recover the money from the employer.

Informing the insurer

An insurer must be told promptly of any claim. This extends to potential claims, not just cases where there has been a formal claim. Different insurers will have different requirements and the employer should make sure that he is aware of the particular insurer's requirements. However, to be safe, an employer should notify his insurer, either directly or through his broker, as soon as there is a possibility of a claim, which probably means as soon as there has been a notifiable accident. The insurer will send a claim form that should be completed as fully as possible and returned promptly. If there is some information that will take a while to collate, send the form back with what information can be given straight away with a covering letter explaining what is to come and when it is hoped that you will be able to send it. The insurer can then say if this timescale is likely to pose a problem.

Ensure that a systematic note is kept of all claims references as failure to give these when writing to insurers will cause delay.

If court proceedings are issued, it is particularly important that the insurer is told straight away, as by that stage strict time limits apply and the insurer may be able to argue that its position has been prejudiced by any delay in forwarding proceedings. Fax, post and/or email the proceedings to the insurers. Sometimes, if a broker has been involved, proceedings may go to the broker first but, in this case, do ensure it is clear that it is the broker's obligation to quickly send the proceedings onto the insurers. Either way, ensure that receipt of the proceedings has been formally acknowledged.

Investigating

An employer will have a record in his accident book of any accident. In all but the most minor cases, it is good practice to investigate any accident fully. It is often helpful to have short witness statements written by those who saw the accident or who otherwise have useful comments, such as the training given, whether usual practices were followed, or whether there was something unusual about the particular task that led to the accident.

The use for these statements is twofold. Firstly and most importantly, it enables a further risk assessment, based on all the information, to be carried out which details the action to be taken to avoid a recurrence of the accident. Secondly, it ensures that accounts of the accident are obtained whilst matters are still fresh in people's minds. Claims may materialise some years after the events in question, by which time it may be too late to take meaningful statements.

Bear in mind, however, that these statements are likely to be disclosable in subsequent civil proceedings if the employer takes them for this dual purpose. Different rules may apply if the insurer investigates an accident solely for the purpose of defending a possible civil claim. In this case, the statements may not be automatically disclosable. If the accident was a serious one, it may be wise to speak to the insurers before doing more than the initial investigations as they may wish to be involved.

Record keeping

A wide range of documents may be relevant to an accident claim and disclosable to a claimant, depending on the circumstances. The claimant may request to see these before the proceedings are issued and is likely to be entitled to do so. Always consult your insurer before disclosing documents to a claimant.

Documents relevant to the accident should be collated and ideally kept in one place or at least a note kept in one place of where the documents may be found. It is important to ensure that these documents are kept, ideally for as long as insurance records have to be kept, i.e. 40 years if no claim has materialised and been dealt with, although it is appreciated that space may well not permit this. Documents should, in any event, be kept for a minimum of five years to allow for the normal three-year limitation period for personal injury claims plus time for any proceedings to be pursued. Again insurers may have specific requirements.

Employers are often surprised to see the documents which they are expected to disclose in a workplace claim. It gives an indication of the onerous duties upon employers and therefore the lists are reproduced in full here. Generally, the following is required:

1.   An accident book entry.

2.   A first aider report.

3.   A surgery record.

4.   A foreman/supervisor's accident report.

5.   A safety representative's accident report.

6.   A RIDDOR report to the HSE.

7.   Other communications between defendants and the HSE.

8.   Minutes of the health and safety committee meeting(s) where the accident/matter was considered.

9.   A report to the DWP.

10. Any documents listed above relating to any previous accident/matter identified by the claimant and relied upon as proof of negligence.

11. Earnings information.

Documents produced to comply with the Management of Health and Safety at Work Regulations 1999

1.   A pre-accident risk assessment

2.   A post-accident re-assessment

3.   An accident investigation report

4. Health surveillance records in appropriate cases

5. Information provided to employees

6. Documents relating to the employees' health and safety training

Disclosure where specific regulations apply

The Workplace (Health, Safety and Welfare) Regulations 1992

1. Repair and maintenance records

2. Housekeeping records

3. Hazard warning signs or notices

The Provision and Use of Work Equipment Regulations 1998 (PUWER)

1. Manufacturers' specifications and instructions in respect of relevant work equipment establishing its suitability

2. Maintenance log/records

3. Documents providing information and instructions to employees

4. Documents provided to the employee in respect of training for use

5. Any notice, sign or document relied upon as a defence to alleged breaches of Regulations 14 to 18 dealing with controls and control systems

6. Instruction/training documents issued to comply with the requirements of Regulation 22 insofar as it deals with maintenance operations where the machinery is not shut down

7. Copies of markings required to comply with Regulation 23

8. Copies of warnings required to comply with Regulation 24

The Personal Protective Equipment at Work Regulations 1992 (PPE)

1. Documents relating to the assessment of personal protective equipment (PPE)

2. Documents relating to the maintenance and replacement of PPE

3. A record of the maintenance procedures for PPE

4. Records of tests and examinations of PPE

5. Documents providing information, instruction and training in relation to PPE

6. Instructions for use of PPE to include the manufacturers' instructions

The Manual Handling Operations Regulations 1992

1. A manual handling risk assessment

2. A re-assessment carried out post-accident

3. Documents showing information provided to the employee giving general indications related to the load and precise indications on the weight of the load and the heaviest side of the load if the centre of gravity was not positioned centrally

4. Documents relating to training in respect of manual handling operations and training records

The Health and Safety (Display Screen Equipment) Regulations 1992 (DSE)

1. An analysis of workstations to assess and reduce risks

2. Re-assessment of the analysis of workstations to assess and reduce risks following the development of symptoms by the claimant

3. Documents detailing the provision of training including training records

4. Documents providing information to employees

The Control of Substances Hazardous to Health Regulations 2002 (COSHH)

1. A risk assessment carried out

2. A reviewed risk assessment carried out.

3. Copy labels from containers used for storage handling and the disposal of carcinogenics

4. Warning signs identifying designation of areas and installations that may be contaminated by carcinogenics

5. Documents relating to the assessment of PPE

6. Documents relating to the maintenance and replacement of PPE

7. A record of maintenance procedures for PPE

8. Records of tests and examinations of PPE

9. Documents providing information, instruction and training in relation to PPE

10. Instructions for use of PPE to include the manufacturers' instructions

11. Air monitoring records for substances assigned a maximum exposure limit or occupational exposure standard

12. A maintenance examination and records of the tests of control measures

13. Monitoring records

14. Health surveillance records

15. Documents detailing information, instruction and training including training records for employees

16. Labels and health and safety data sheets supplied to the employers

The Construction (Design and Management) Regulations 2007

1. A Notification of Project Form (HSE F10)

2. A health and safety plan

3. A health and safety file

4.   Information and training records

5.   Records of advice from, and views of, persons at work

The Pressure Systems Safety Regulations 2000

1.   Information and specimen markings

2.   Written statements specifying the safe operating limits of a system

3.   A copy of the written scheme of examination

4.   Examination records

5.   Instructions provided for the use of the operator

6.   Records kept to comply with the requirements of Regulation 13

7.   Records kept to comply with the requirements of Regulation 22

The Noise at Work Regulations 1989 and The Control of Noise at Work Regulations 2005

1.   Any risk assessment records, findings and plans

2.   Manufacturers' literature in respect of all ear protection made available to the claimant

3.   All documents provided to the employee for the provision of information to comply with Regulation 10 of the 2005 Regulations

The Personal Protective Equipment Regulations 2002 (PPE)

1.   A pre-accident assessment of head protection

2.   A post-accident re-assessment

Giving evidence

This can be an alarming experience even for the best prepared witness. In a large case, the witness may have had an opportunity to meet the solicitor dealing with the case and discuss any concerns. He also may have seen the barrister instructed. In a smaller case, the employer, or a representative of the insurer, may have taken the witness statement and the first the witness sees of the legal representatives is at the court door. The following guidelines may help.

Guidance on being a witness

- **Tell the truth.** Remember that in cross-examination the advocate on the other side will be trying to make you admit things in his side's favour. Do not change your story to suit what you think helps your version of events. It will be obvious and you will lose credibility.

- **Remember that you are at court to give evidence.** You are not there to win the case and you are not on trial; you are there to assist the judge.

- **Arrive in good time.** Ideally go and see a court in action before you have to give evidence.

- **Keep calm.** Take your time.

- **Listen carefully to the questions being asked.** Take time to think before answering. You will not get a second chance.

- **Ask for a question to be repeated if you do not understand it.** The judge will understand that a lawyer's language can be confusing to the most intelligent people.

- **Speak up.** The acoustics can be poor in a court room.

- **Look at the judge when speaking.**

- **Keep your answers short.** If more information is needed, you will be asked for it.

- **Be polite.** The judge and lawyers will normally try to be as polite as possible to you. You will make a better impression if you are polite in return.

- **Keep your temper.** Do not take things personally. Concentrate on giving your evidence.

- **Ask for a copy of a document if you are being asked questions about it.**

- **Be serious.** Do not try to be funny as it is likely to backfire.

- **Dress smartly.** People in court are normally formally dressed. You do not want to feel or look out of place.

Control of the case

Generally, insurers will effectively be in control of the case and will normally have the right to make key decisions if necessary without the agreement of the insured, under the terms of the policy. If it is important to an employer that a certain line is taken on a case or if, for example, settlement of one claim may have wider implications and may lead to many others, it is important that the insurer is clearly informed of this at an early stage.

The employer must co-operate with his insurers, allow time for witnesses to be interviewed and do his best to ensure that witnesses attend court when required.

4.5 Defending HSE and local authority prosecutions

From 2012 to 2013, the Health and Safety Executive (HSE) prosecuted 574 cases with a conviction rate of 95 per cent. Some organisations were prosecuted for more than one offence relating to an incident. The HSE prosecuted 973 health and safety offences with a conviction rate of 87 per cent.

In recent years, there have been large increases in the level of financial penalties following successful prosecutions. The average fine per case between 2012 and 2013 was £15,153 per offence. Companies are more likely than ever to be prosecuted, to be convicted and to receive significant fines.

Accidents do happen and when they do, the difference between a company being prosecuted or simply being issued with a warning will depend upon whether proper care and attention has previously been given to the implementation of a thorough, well-considered, health and safety policy. This would include safe systems of work, safe plant, equipment and machinery, the adequate supervision of employees and properly conducted risk assessments.

But in the event that the HSE do seek to prosecute a company (or indeed an individual), there are steps which can be taken to limit the extent of the financial penalties that typically follow convictions in such proceedings.

Legal advice

It is vital to obtain legal advice at an early stage. Your insurance company may cover you for the legal costs of defending a health and safety prosecution, but not the fine or prosecution costs should you be found guilty. Ensure that your solicitors have specialist experience in health and safety prosecutions.

Advance disclosure

Before a company has to inform the Magistrates' Court whether or not it is going to plead guilty or not guilty to a particular charge, the company is entitled to the disclosure of detailed information setting out the case against it, including the relevant documents and statements.

Always consider this information first before deciding on how you, or your company, intend to plead; your legal advisers will be able to assist you with this decision.

Which court?

Once you, or the company, has informed the Magistrates' Court whether you intend to plead guilty or not guilty, the magistrates will determine whether the case will be heard in the Magistrates' Court or in the Crown Court. It is important to obtain legal advice as to which court your case should be heard in.

Defence/mitigation

Your legal adviser will inform you how to defend yourself against an HSE prosecution or at least reduce the penalty imposed. However, do bear the following in mind:

- It is important to demonstrate to the court all, or any, of the company's efforts, since the day of the accident, to address any deficiencies in the company's health and safety policy.

- All health and safety documentation should be produced including copies of accident reports, any communications with the HSE and any risk assessments, as well as the company's health and safety policy.

- A health and safety consultant may assist the company in assessing the workplace after the accident and may make appropriate suggestions as to how systems can be improved. Evidence can then be provided to the court as to the timescale within which you, as employer, propose to implement the health and safety consultant's recommendations.

- As with any criminal proceedings, a level of remorse is usually appreciated by the court and any admissions, or partial admissions, will often reduce the level and nature of the penalty.

- Properly audited accounts for the previous three to five years should be provided to the court in the event that a fine is considered.

Penalties

The Health and Safety (Offences) Act 2008 came into force on 16 January 2009. It does not apply to offences committed prior to this date. The Act revises the mode of trial and maximum penalties applicable to certain offences relating to health and safety. It has amended Schedule 3A of the HSW Act. The most notable changes are that more offences carry the maximum fine of £20,000 in the Magistrates' Court. The Magistrates' Court now has the power in some cases to impose a six-month custodial sentence as well as a fine and the Crown Court can impose a two-year custodial sentence for a greater number of offences. There is no limit on the aggregate fine that can be imposed in respect of a number of different offences. In the Crown Court the fines can be unlimited.

The effect of the Act is to increase financial penalties but it also means that more offences are capable of being dealt with by the Magistrates' Court. Although there are greater powers to impose a custodial sentence the Court Sentencing Guidelines stress that custodial sentences should be reserved for the most serious cases where culpability and the risk of harm are high.

The courts consider a number of factors in every case:

1. Death resulting from any breach (regardless of how minor the breach) must be regarded as an aggravating factor.

2. It is considered a serious aggravating factor if the defendant has deliberately profited from a failure to take necessary health and safety measures, or ran a risk to save money.

3. Failure to heed warnings is considered to be an aggravating factor. Such warnings range from formal advice from the HSE, to the occurrence of similar incidents in the past, concerns raised by employers or even events which might have given warnings to the employer.

4. In assessing the gravity of the breach, the court must consider how far short the defendant fell from doing what was reasonably practicable.

5. The degree of risk and the extent of the danger created by the offence must be considered in every case.

6. The court will consider the extent of the breach, i.e. whether it was an isolated incident or if it had been continuing for a period of time and whether there have been previous offences of a similar nature.

7. In the company's favour the court will take into account the following:

   (a) Whether a prompt admission of responsibility was made and a quick plea of guilty.

   (b) What steps were taken to remedy deficiencies after they were drawn to the defendant's attention.

   (c) A good previous safety record.

   (d) Cooperation with the regulatory authorities.

The level of any fine should not only reflect the gravity of the offence but also the means of the offender and this applies as much to companies as to individuals.

If a defendant company wishes to make any submissions to the court about the appropriate level of the fine and its ability to pay such a fine, it should supply copies of its accounts and any other financial information on which it intends to rely, in good time before the court hearing, to both the court and to the prosecution. If a company does not produce its accounts, the court can assume that the company can pay whatever fine the court imposes.

Prosecution costs

Where a person or company is convicted of an offence, the court may make a costs order against the defendant. Costs are more of an issue in health and safety cases than in other criminal cases, as the costs incurred can be much higher. However, costs orders should never exceed a sum which the company or individual is able to pay, having regards to his means and to any fine imposed on him.

Defence costs

If the charges against you are withdrawn, you are acquitted or you successfully appeal a health and safety prosecution you should be awarded your defence costs. The government tried to introduce a scheme limiting defence costs to legal aid rates with the Costs in Criminal Cases (General) (Amendments) Regulations 2009 which took effect from 31 October 2009 but this was ruled unlawful. Costs will be assessed based on reasonableness.

4.6 **Corporate manslaughter**

Corporate manslaughter is a crime committed by an organisation when it causes the death of those to which it owed a duty of care. The Corporate Manslaughter and Corporate Homicide Act 2007 ('the Act') came into force in the whole of the UK on 6 April 2008, and it replaces the previous offence of gross negligent manslaughter. It does not apply to individuals who remain liable under existing health and safety legislation and common law.

To be found guilty, the way the organisation's senior management arranged its activities must have grossly breached its duty of care and resulted in a fatality. In determining whether a gross breach has occurred, a jury must consider whether the organisation also breached health and safety legislation, how serious the failure was, and how much of a risk there was of death occurring. In addition, the jury can take into account the attitudes, policies and accepted practices of the organisation to identify whether there was a defective health and safety system in place. The penalty is an unlimited fine, but the court can also require the organisation to publicise its conviction, or to take steps to remedy its failures.

The difficulty with the previous law of gross negligent manslaughter was that an organisation could only be convicted if a senior individual – a 'controlling mind' – of the organisation was found guilty of manslaughter. One such rare conviction was the case of R v Kite and OLL Ltd. Peter Kite was the managing director of OLL, an outdoor activity company operating out of Lyme Bay. When four students drowned on a canoeing trip in the bay, Mr Kite and the company, OLL, were both convicted of gross negligent manslaughter. He was a 'controlling mind', given that he was the sole director of the company and was therefore responsible for devising, implementing and enforcing a suitable health and safety policy.

However, the requirement for a 'controlling mind' does not accurately reflect the reality of the modern large corporation, where health and safety responsibility is often delegated to junior staff, and it is unlikely that one person could be said to embody the organisation in his actions. This meant that only seven small companies were successfully prosecuted under the previous offence, and larger corporations managed to escape liability.

In addition to a prosecution for corporate manslaughter, the organisation can also be prosecuted for breaching health and safety legislation. If the organisation is found guilty of both offences, it could face two unlimited fines. Individuals can also still be found guilty of gross negligent manslaughter if they are personally to blame. The Act essentially targets reckless organisations with no regard for health and safety, as if it can be shown that reasonable safeguards and a robust approach to safety were in place when the death(s) occurred, the organisation will not be guilty of corporate manslaughter.

The new offence would probably now mean that organisations such as P&O Ferries, the company who operated the Herald of Free Enterprise ferry, could now be held responsible for occurrences such as the Zeebrugge disaster. In that case, due to the law as it previously stood, the judge was unable to find that a sufficiently senior member of the management was grossly negligent to enable him to hold the company liable. The position will remain much the same as before for smaller organisations and therefore the previous imbalance between small and large organisations should be redressed. There have so far been four convictions for corporate manslaughter under the Act. The first conviction involved a company called Cotswold Geotechnical Holdings Ltd. They were convicted and fined £385,000 when an employee died after an unsupported pit he was working in collapsed. The company was run by a sole director, who was on-site just before the incident. It remains to be determined how effective the Act will be when a prosecution is made against a large company.

Sentencing for corporate manslaughter and health and safety offences causing death

Cases involving fatalities will usually be dealt with in the Crown Court and will attract a higher fine in any event. However, fines where fatalities have occurred have also been increasing. On 9 February 2010, the Sentencing Guidelines Council published its definitive guideline for 'Corporate Manslaughter and Health and Safety Offences Causing Death'. The Guideline applies to the sentencing of organisations on or after 15 February 2010 for first offences, where it is proved that the offence was a significant cause of death.

The Guideline states that for the offence of corporate manslaughter, the appropriate fine will seldom be less than £500,000 and may be millions of pounds. Thus far however, none of the fines have exceeded this figure. It states that where a breach of health and safety legislation has caused death, the appropriate fine will seldom be less than £100,000 and may be hundreds of thousands of pounds or more. It states that when assessing the level of fine, the court should consider the means of the organisation, the effect on employment of the innocent, provision of services to the public and whether the fine will put the defendant out of business, although in some bad cases this may be an acceptable consequence. The effect on shareholders, directors, prices and liability to pay civil compensation will not normally be relevant.

In the case of a large organisation the fine should be payable within 28 days. In the case of a smaller or financially stretched organisation it is permissible to allow payment to spread over a much longer period.

The court can also impose a Remedial Order requiring the organisation to remedy any specific failings involved in the offence. However, the organisation ought to have already remedied any problems before sentencing to assist mitigation. For offences of corporate manslaughter only, the court can impose a Publicity Order requiring publication of the conviction, particulars of the offence, the amount of the fine and the terms of any Remedial Order.

Points for action

- Consider appointing a director responsible for health and safety, as well as a committee, to assist.

- Hold regular meetings and ensure that fellow directors are au fait with the decisions and practices.

- Consider who in the organisation would qualify as senior management and review job titles to ensure that senior management is accurately identified.

- Review the following:

  - The organisation's safety culture – attitudes count as well as policies. Ensure that employees are comfortable reporting health and safety incidents.

  - Industry standards and sector specific codes of practice to ensure compliance.

  - All risk assessments to ensure that they are up to date.

  - The organisation's policies, procedures and near miss reports.

  - Revisit (or write) a disaster management plan to ensure that there is a protocol for dealing with authorities and working with legal advisers if a fatality occurs.

- Check the extent of the organisation's insurance cover for potential liability under the new offence.

- For manufacturers and suppliers, the offence is also relevant to fatalities as a result of the supply of alleged defective goods. Check that there is a system ensuring that safety and quality checks are carried out on all supplied parts and ingredients, as well as the 'finished product', with a clear procedure in place for product recall.

Appendices

Useful addresses

Association of British Insurers (ABI)

Employers' Liability Enquiry Unit
51 Gresham Street
London EC2V 7HQ

Tel: 020 7600 3333
Email: info@abi.org.uk
Website: www.abi.org.uk

Association of Noise Consultants

Airport House
Purley Way
Croydon CR0 0XZ

Tel: 020 8253 4518
Email: mail@association-of-
noise-consultants.co.uk
Website: www.association-of-
noise-consultants.co.uk

British Red Cross

44 Moorfields
London EC2Y 9AL

Tel: 0844 871 1111
Email: information@redcross.org.uk
Website: www.redcross.org.uk

British Safety Council

70 Chancellors Road
London W6 9RS

Tel: 020 3510 8355
Email: customer.service@britsafe.org
Website: www.britsafe.org

British Standards Institution (BSI Group)

BSI Sales and Customer Services
389 Chiswick High Road
London W4 4AL

Tel: 020 8996 9000
Email: cservices@bsigroup.com
Website: www.bsigroup.co.uk

BUPA Wellness Service

15-19 Bloomsbury Way
London WC1A 2BA

Tel: 08081 634 545 (personal)
Tel: 03452 668 974 (business)
Website: www.bupa.co.uk

Centre for Stress Management

156 Westcombe Hill
London SE3 7DH

Tel: 0845 680 2065
Email: admin@iafpd.com
Website: www.managing
stress.com

Citizens Advice

3rd Floor North
200 Aldersgate Street
London EC1A 4HD

Tel: 0300 0231 231 (admin only)
Website: www.citizensadvice.
org.uk

Criminal Injuries Compensation Authority

Alexander Bain House
15 York Street
Glasgow G2 8JQ

Tel: 0300 003 3601
Website: www.cica.gov.uk

Disability Unit

Benefit Enquiry Line for people with disabilities: 0845 712 3456
Email: BEL-Customer-
Services@dwp.gsi.gov.uk
Website: www.disability.gov.uk

Equality Advisory and Support Service

FREEPOST
Equality Advisory Support Service
FPN4431

Tel: 0808 800 0082
Website: www.equalityadvisory
service.com

The Financial Conduct Authority (FCA)

25 The North Colonnade
Canary Wharf
London E14 5HS

Tel: 020 7066 1000
Email: consumer.queries@fca.org.uk
Website: www.fca.org.uk

Fire Training Videos Limited

110 Warren Road Worthing West Sussex BN14 9QX	Tel: 01903 268 000 Email: info@firetraining videos.com Website: www.firetraining videos.com

HSE Books

PO Box 1999 Sudbury Suffolk CO10 2WA	Tel: 01787 881 165 Email: hsebooks@prolog.uk.com Website: books.hse.gov.uk

Health & Safety Executive (HSE)

Website: www.hse.gov.uk

Institute of Occupational Safety and Health (IOSH)

The Grange Highfield Drive Wigston Leicestershire LE18 1NN	Tel: 0116 257 3100 Website: www.iosh.co.uk

International Institute of Risk and Safety Management (IIRSM)

Suite 7a 77 Fulham Palace Road London W6 8JA	Tel: 020 8741 9100 Email: info@iirsm.org Website: www.iirsm.org

Ministry of Justice

102 Petty France London SW1H 9AJ	Tel: 020 3334 3555 Email: general.queries@justice. gsi.gov.uk Website: www.justice.gov.uk Civil Procedure Rules link: www. justice.gov.uk/civil/procrules_fin

Motor Insurers' Bureau

Linford Wood House
6–12 Capital Drive
Linford Wood
Milton Keynes MK14 6XT

Tel: 01908 830 001
Email: enquiries@mib.org.uk
Website: www.miic.org.uk

Prudential Regulation Authority

Bank of England
Threadneedle Street
London EC2R 8AH

Tel: 020 7601 4878
Email: enquiries@bankofengland.
co.uk
Website: www.bankofengland.
co.uk

Royal Society for the Prevention of Accidents (RoSPA)

RoSPA House
28 Calthorpe Road
Edgbaston
Birmingham B15 1RP

Tel: 0121 248 2000
Email: help@rospa.com
Website: www.rospa.com

St Andrew's Ambulance Association

St. Andrew's House
48 Milton Street
Glasgow G4 0HR

Tel: 0141 332 4031
Email: glasgow@firstaid.org.uk
Website: www.firstaid.org.uk

St John Ambulance

27 St John's Lane
London EC1M 4BU

Tel: 08700 104950
Website: www.sja.org.uk

Solicitors Regulation Authority

The Cube
199 Wharfside Street
Birmingham B1 1RN

Tel: 0370 606 2555
Website: www.sra.org.uk

Stationery Office (formerly HMSO)

St Crispins	Tel: 01603 622211
Duke Street	Website: www.tso.co.uk
Norwich NR3 1PD	

Trades Union Congress (TUC)

Congress House	Tel: 020 7636 4030
Great Russell Street	Website: www.tuc.org.uk
London WC1B 3LS	

Useful publications

Most of the following publications can be purchased on the Health and Safety Executive's website at www.hsebooks.com or on the British Standards Institution's website at http://shop.bsigroup.com.

The health and safety publication abbreviations mean the following:

ACOP	Approved Code of Practice
BS	British Standard
EH	Guidance Note: Environmental health
HSE	Health and Safety Executive leaflet
HSG	Health and Safety (Guidance) booklet
INDG	Industry Advisory (General) leaflet
INDS	Industry Advisory (Special) leaflet
ISBN	International Standard Book Numbers
L	Legal series

Chapter 2

'First aiders' (page 14)

- Posters: *Basic Advice on First Aid at Work* (ISBN 9780717661930) – £5.00 for 10 copies – and *Electric Shock: First Aid Procedures* (ISBN 9780717664337) – £12.50 each

'The health and safety policy document' (page 18)

- *Health and Safety made simple* (INDG449)

'Risk assessments' (page 24)

- *Risk Assessment eKit* available from www.lawpack.co.uk
- *A Guide to Risk Assessment Requirements: Common Provisions in Health and Safety Law* (INDG218)

Chapter 3

'Manual handling' (page 49)

- *Manual Handling at work* (INDG143REV3)

'VDUs' (page 58)

- *Working with VDUs* (INDG36 rev 2)

'Noise' (page 83)

- *Noise at Work: Advice for Employers* (INDG362 rev 2)

'Vibration' (page 86)

- *Vibration Solutions: Practical Ways to Reduce the Risk of Hand-Arm Vibration Injury* (HSG170)
- *Health Risks From Hand-Arm Vibration: Advice for Employees and the Self-Employed* (INDG126REV1)

'Machinery' (page 93)

- *Guidance on safe use of machinery* (PD5304:2005)

Statutes

- Coroners and Justice Act 2009
- Corporate Manslaughter and Corporate Homicide Act 2007
- Employer's Liability (Compulsory Insurance) Act 1969
- Enterprise and Regulatory Reform Act 2013
- Environmental Protection Act 1990
- Equality Act 2010
- Fire Precautions Act 1971
- Health Act 2006
- Health and Safety at Work Act 1974
- Health and Safety (Offences) Act 2008
- Mesothelioma Act 2014
- Occupiers' Liability Act 1957
- Trade Union Reform and Employment Rights Act 1993

Regulations

- The Agency Workers Regulations 2010
- The Agency Workers (Amendment) Regulations 2011
- The Conduct of Employment Agencies and Employment Businesses Regulations 2003
- The Construction (Design and Management) Regulations 1994
- The Construction (Design and Management) Regulations 2007
- The Construction (General Provisions) Regulations 1961
- The Construction (Head Protection) Regulations 1989 (now revoked)
- The Construction (Health and Safety) Regulations 1996
- The Construction (Design and Management) Regulations 2015
- The Control of Asbestos Regulations 2012
- The Control of Noise at Work Regulations 2005
- The Control of Substances Hazardous to Health Regulations 2002 (COSHH)
- The Control of Vibration at Work Regulations 2005
- The Costs in Criminal Cases (General amendments) Regulations 2009
- The Diffuse Mesothelioma Payment Scheme (Amendment) Regulations 2015
- The Electricity at Work Regulations 1989
- The Employer's Liability (Compulsory Insurance) Regulations 1998
- The Health and Safety at Work Regulations 1999
- The Health and Safety (Consultation with Employees) Regulations 1996
- The Health and Safety (Display Screen Equipment) Regulations 1992 (DSE) – Guidance on Regulations (L26)
- The Health and Safety (Fees) Regulations 2012
- The Health and Safety (First Aid) Regulations 1981
- The Health and Safety Information for Employees Regulations 1989
- The Health and Safety (Safety Signs and Signals) Regulations 1996
- The Ionising Radiations (Outside Workers) Regulations 1993
- The Ionising Radiations Regulations 1999
- The Lifting Operations and Lifting Equipment Regulations 1998 (LOLER) – Approved Code of Practice and Guidance (L113)
- The Lifting Plant and Equipment (Records of Test and Examination etc) Regulations 1992
- The Management of Health and Safety at Work (Amendment) Regulations 2006

- The Management of Health and Safety at Work Regulations 1999
- The Managing Construction for Health and Safety (CDM Regulations) 2007 – Approved Code of Practice (L144)
- The Manual Handling Operations Regulations 1992 – Guidance on Regulations (L23)
- The Mesothelioma Lump Sum Payments (Conditions and Amounts) (Amendment) Regulations 2015) 1989
- The Noise at Work Regulations 1989
- The Personal Protective Equipment at Work Regulations 1992 (PPE) – Guidance on Regulations (L25)
- The Pressure Systems Safety Regulations 2000
- The Provision and Use of Work Equipment Regulations 1998 (PUWER)
- The Registration, Evaluation and Authorisation of Chemicals Regulations (Regulation (EC) No 1907/2006)
- The Regulatory Reform (Fire Safety) Order 2005
- The Reporting of Injuries, Diseases and Dangerous Occurrences Regulations 2013 (RIDDOR) – Guidance on Regulations (L73)
- The Safety Signs Regulations 1996
- The Safe Use of Work Equipment Provision and Use of Work Equipment Regulations 1998 – Approved Code of Practice and Guidance on Regulations (L22)
- The Safety Representatives and Safety Committees Regulations 1977
- The Smoke-free (Premises and Enforcement) Regulations 2006
- The Smoke-free (Signs) Regulations 2012
- The Smoke-free (Exemptions and Vehicles) Regulations 2007
- The Smoke-free (Penalties and Discounted Amounts) Regulations 2007
- The Smoke-free (Vehicle operators and Penalty notices) regulations 2007
- The Work at Height Regulations 2005
- The Working Time (Amendment)Regulations 2003
- The Workplace (Health, Safety and Welfare) Regulations 1992 – Approved Code of Practice and Guidance on Regulations (L24)

Work-related diseases and their causes

Diseases/ conditions	Possible causes	Description of disease/condition
Alveolitis	Exposure to moulds, fungal spores or heterologous proteins during work in: 1. agriculture, horticulture, forestry, cultivation of edible fungi or malt-working; 2. loading, unloading or handling mouldy vegetable matter or edible fungi whilst it is being stored; 3. caring for or handling birds.	Inflammation of the alveoli of the lungs caused by an allergic reaction. When caused by infection, it is called pneumonia, when caused by a chemical/ physical agent, it is called pneumonitis. Farmer's Lung – form of this caused by inhalation of dust from mouldy hay/ straw.
Angiosarcoma	Work in or about machinery or apparatus used for the polymerisation of vinyl chloride monomer.	A highly malignant tumour.
Anthrax	1. Work involving handling infected animals, their products or packaging containing infected material; or 2. Work on infected sites.	A usually fatal, acute infection.
Asbestosis	Caused by inhalation of mainly blue or brown asbestos dust, either during mining or quarrying, or in one of the many industries in which it is used (e.g. in the making of paper, cardboard and brake linings, and as an insulating material).	Widespread scarring in the lungs leading to severe breathing difficulties.

Diseases/ conditions	Possible causes	Description of disease/condition
Barotrauma	Work involving breathing gases at increased pressure (including diving).	Non-infective inflammatory changes produced in the ear.
Brucellosis	Work involving contact with: 1. animals or their carcasses; or 2. laboratory specimens or vaccines of or containing brucella.	Undulating fever, drenching sweats, pains in joints and back and headache.
Bursitis	Physically demanding work causing severe or prolonged friction or pressure at or about the knee.	Inflammation of the knee or shoulder.
Byssinosis	The spinning or manipulation of raw or waste cotton or flax or the weaving of cotton or flax.	Pneumoconiosis/ chronic inflammatory thickening of lung tissue due to inhalation of dust.
Carcinoma	Any occupation in: 1. glass manufacture; 2. sandstone tunnelling or quarrying; 3. the pottery industry; 4. metal ore mining; 5. slate quarrying or slate production; 6. clay mining; 7. the use of siliceous materials as abrasives; 8. foundry work; 9. granite tunnelling or quarrying; or 10. stone cutting or masonry.	Any cancer.

Diseases/ conditions	Possible causes	Description of disease/condition
Carpal tunnel syndrome	Work involving the use of hand-held vibrating tools. Is also constitutional.	Attacks of pain and tingling in the first three or four fingers of one/both hands, usually at night. Caused by pressure on the median nerve.
Cataract	Work involving exposure to electromagnetic radiation (including radiant heat).	An opacity of the lens. A cataract may be the result of a penetrating or blunt injury, infra-red energy, electric shock or ionizing radiation.
Chrome ulcer	Caused by chromic acid which is used in several industries, particularly in chromium plating.	Deep ulcer, particularly of the nasal septum and knuckles.
Dysbaric osteonecrosis	Work involving breathing gases at increased pressure (including diving).	Death of the mass of bone (osteonecrosis).
Legionellosis	Work on or near cooling systems which are located in the workplace and use water; or work on hot water service systems located in the workplace which are likely to be a source of contamination.	Form of pneumonia due to bacterium distributed in nature and commonly found in surface water and soil. Aches and pains followed rapidly by a rise in temperature, shivering attacks, coughing and shortness in breath.

Diseases/ conditions	Possible causes	Description of disease/condition
Leptospirosis	1. Work in places which are, or are liable to be, infested by rats, fieldmice, voles or other small mammals; 2. Work at dog kennels or involving the care or handling of dogs; or	Disease caused by a group of micro-organisms normally found in rodents and other small mammals. Varies from a mild
	3. Work involving contact with bovine animals or their meat products, or pigs or their meat products.	influenza-like illness to a fatal form of jaundice due to severe liver disease. Kidneys often involved.
Lyme disease	Work involving exposure to ticks (including, in particular, work by forestry workers, rangers, dairy farmers, gamekeepers and other persons engaged in countryside management).	Comprises of arthritis associated with skin rashes, fever, encephalitis or inflammation of the heart. Transmitted by tick bites.
Mesothelioma	1. The working or handling of asbestos or any mixture of asbestos; or 2. The manufacture or repair of asbestos textiles or other articles containing or composed of asbestos.	Malignant tumour of the pleura, the membrane lining of the chest cavity. May be asymptomatic or cause pain/coughing/breathing trouble.
Peripheral neuropathy	Work involving the use or handling of, or exposure to, the fumes of or vapour containing n-hexane or methyl n-butyl ketone.	Disease affecting the nerves.

Diseases/ conditions	Possible causes	Description of disease/condition
Pneumoco-niosis	1. The mining, quarrying or working of silica rock or the working of dried quartzose sand, or any dry deposit or residue of silica or any dry mixture containing such materials; or 2. The breaking, crushing or grinding of flint; or 3. Sand blasting by means of compressed air with the use of quartzose sand or crushed silica rock or flint; or 4. Working in a foundry; or 5. The manufacture of china or earthenware; or 6. The grinding of mineral graphite; or 7. The dressing of granite or any igneous rock by masons; or 8. Working underground in any mine.	General name applied to a chronic form of inflammation of the lungs.
Q Fever	Work involving contact with animals, their remains or their untreated products.	Fever, severe headache and often pneumonia. Disease due to organism *Coxiella burnetii*.
Streptococcus	Work involving contact with pigs infected with streptococcus.	Variety of bacterium.

Diseases/ conditions	Possible causes	Description of disease/condition
Tennis elbow	Any job involving the jarring/ straining of the elbow.	Mild inflammation in the tendons or muscles in the elbow.
Tenosynovitis	Any job involving jarring/ straining/repetitive movements.	Inflammation of a tendon.
Tinnitus	Any job involving exposure to noise.	Noise heard in the ear is a frequent accompaniment of deafness caused by damage to the auditory pathway.

Pandemics – Swine flu

Employers and employees should already be practising good personal hygiene in the workplace to prevent diseases from spreading. Two key examples are the slogan 'Catch it. Bin it. Kill it.' in relation to capturing sneezes in tissues and the importance of employees washing their hands after going to the lavatory and before eating and drinking. However, since the arrival of swine flu in the UK, there are now extra measures that should be taken. Employers should:

- Advise workers to stay at home if they have flu-like symptoms and they have good reason to believe (referring to Health Protection Agency (HPA) guidance) that they may have been exposed to swine flu.
- Send home employees who are experiencing flu-like symptoms and who have good reason to believe (again referring to HPA guidance) that they may have been exposed to swine flu.

Further information about swine flu can be found on the HPA website www.hpa.org.uk.

Temperature

As the climate becomes more extreme, with long hot summers and cold wet winters, employers should pay increasing attention to the requirements regarding temperature in the workplace. In an indoor workplace, employers must provide:

- a reasonable working temperature of at least 16°C although 13°C is acceptable if the working conditions are strenuous and the law may require certain workplaces to have lower temperatures;
- cooling or heating systems in cases where a reasonable working temperature cannot be maintained (note these must not emit hazardous or unpleasant levels of fumes);
- enough space in offices, i.e. no cramped conditions; and
- thermal clothing and rest facilities if necessary, i.e. for working in hot or cold temperatures.

For more detailed information on temperature in the workplace, such as heat and cold stress, dehydration and outdoor working, please visit the HSE website at www.hse.gov.uk.

Index

Allen Carr

The easy way for
women
to
lose
weight

ARCTURUS

To our amazing team of Senior Allen Carr's Easyway Therapists around the world

Thanks also to Tim Glynne-Jones for additional editorial input

ARCTURUS

This edition published in 2017 by Arcturus Publishing Limited
26/27 Bickels Yard, 151–153 Bermondsey Street,
London SE1 3HA, UK

ISBN: 978-1-78599-303-9
AD004834UK

Printed in the UK